# DETOURS &
# DREAMS

# DETOURS &
# DREAMS

## FINDING HOPE, HELP, & ANSWERS

KATHY HENIGAN JIMERSON

WESTBOW
PRESS®
A DIVISION OF THOMAS NELSON
& ZONDERVAN

WestBow Press books may be ordered through booksellers or by contacting:

WestBow Press
A Division of Thomas Nelson & Zondervan
1663 Liberty Drive
Bloomington, IN 47403
www.westbowpress.com
1 (866) 928-1240

ISBN: 978-1-9736-5369-1 (sc)
ISBN: 978-1-9736-5370-7 (hc)
ISBN: 978-1-9736-5368-4 (e)

Library of Congress Control Number: 2019901656

Print information available on the last page.

WestBow Press rev. date: 2/28/2019

# CONTENTS

Dedicated to the older, wiser women who came into my life when I needed what only they could give. Because of their unconditional love and continual encouragement, I found who I was meant to be. They were and are my blessings.

# INTRODUCTION

Growing up, I was called a "storyteller." Whether riding the school bus or just hanging out with friends, kids loved my stories. I made them up on the spot; no rhyme, reason, just tall tales woven with sheer fun and imagination, hoping there would be a punch line because just like my captive audience, I had no clue where I was going. My stories never failed to draw a crowd, and someone would say, "You made that whole thing up," whereas I'd laughed and say, "Maybe I did, but you believed it." It was fun, and for a short while, I felt important and the center of their attention.

I'm no longer a young kid, nor do I tell tall tales except to my grandkids, who believe every word of them. But there is still a story to be told. It's no tall tale; it's real. All of it is true, even when I wished it wasn't.

It's worth telling because there's a whole group of people out there who need to hear it. So I'm not telling for me; I'm telling it for them. Maybe you are one of those people.

You see, sometimes as kids, we do things that turn us and our families upside down and inside out. We lose the core of who we are, or maybe, for the first time, we discover we really never knew who we were in the first place. Your bags get packed with guilt, shame, hopelessness, and lots of fear that the future just shut its doors; you pick up those heavy bags and begin to live out of them. No one tells you differently; some even tell you this is who you are now.

Out of the blue, one by one, some older women are sprinkled like pixy dust along your desolate journey. But unlike pixy dust, their words, actions, and unconditional love go deep into your wounded heart, and like a key in a dull rusty lock, the door opens, and you come out of that self-made prison.

The journey is still hard, the challenges tough, but for the first time, you see differently. You're not sure why; you just know the sky is blue, the grass is green, and you are different. Just as those women made a difference in you without realizing it, you are going to do the same for the ones placed on your path. Some call it paying it forward; I just call it doing for others what they did for me.

This is my story. I've waited a long time to tell it, but too many people are letting others write their story for them. I met some of those people; once I was one of those people.

There's an old saying; "Keep doing the same thing the same way, and you get the same results." I remember saying that to a group of kids who were living with some grown-up responsibilities. Then I asked a question no one had: What are you going to do differently? Silence; you don't often combine a room full of teenagers and silence, but that day was different.

They knew my story; they knew why I was doing what I was doing for them, but they needed more than my story and a motivational talk. They needed to know how to turn their lives around.

Together, on that day so long ago, I paid it forward.

Through my story and some of their stories, we want to help you, teenagers and parents alike, unpack those heavy suitcases and find the life, purpose, and future that belongs to you.

# THE BREAKTHROUGH

In the same instance my hand reached for the door, I immediately pulled it back. I didn't want to be here; anywhere but here. The musty smell of old wood and indoor/outdoor carpet aged with years of wear caused me to step back and take another breath of air; I just wanted to turn and run. It took courage to do this; I didn't have that courage. Not today; not ever.

It began when another teacher innocently asked, "Will you speak to my class? They really need a pep talk." In a moment of weakness, I had agreed; for the next several days, I regretted it and wanted desperately to back out. I was new to this school district as well as this particular job and not really sure what to do or where to start. Somehow, a motivational pep talk wasn't at the top of my list, but here I was. I felt queasy; I had never spoken to a group of any kind, but especially not to a group like this.

I didn't have far to travel. My office was housed in an old portable building adjoining this out-of-the-way classroom. Weathered planks guided my steps down a long narrow hallway, creaking with each step. There could be no unannounced visitors, that's for sure. The only people who knew this classroom was even here were the ones who needed to know. It was definitely tucked out of sight. One teacher covered all subjects. Only girls went here. They often ranged from thirteen to eighteen. It wasn't a typical one-room schoolhouse. In some ways, this room was a shelter, a temporary refuge from mainstream education.

As I stood paralyzed with my hand on the doorknob, beads of sweat slid down my temples; my heart was racing, yet I knew there was no turning back. I said yes. Better than most, I understood the power of yes. Such a simple word, yet so life-changing. When I told the teacher yes, I made a commitment; I made a choice. That is what yes does.

When I walked through the door and into their lives, I got a cold, uninviting reception. The teacher told them I was coming, and to them, I probably looked like another do-gooder with some warm, fuzzy, feel-good words. Their faces were locked in unison; they didn't want me there. No one made eye contact. Some stared at the floor; others stared out the window, but no one looked at me. It would have been easy to turn around and walk—or run— out the door.

Scanning the sea of faces left me reeling with the reality of my own memories, where I had once been. This was all too close and way too personal. Perspiring like a melting ice sculpture, I leaned against a desk as my knees buckled.

No boys were present, although they were well represented; you might say they were the silent partners. Only girls in this room. The shock of so many was disturbing; a quick look revealed almost twenty teenage girls. The ages were mixed; some were as young as middle school. Age, culture, or affluence didn't discriminate. Sizes and shapes varied. They had one thing in common: They were pregnant. Some would keep their babies, some would choose adoption. Eventually, one by one, they would return to their normal school, where "normal" would never be normal again. They would all be mothers.

I was quickly losing what little courage I had mustered.

*They don't need a pep talk. They need someone to care enough to tell them the truth.*

I knew that voice, and I also knew I was the only one hearing it. Ever since I had asked Jesus Christ into my life, I was becoming more accustomed to that inner conversation. While it usually gave me a form of peace, I was often encouraged to step outside my comfort zone and do things I didn't want to do.

I knew this was one of those times.

My mind raced back to the earlier days, when I wished someone had been there for me when I felt alone and condemned; when a boulder of hopelessness tried to bury all possibility for a future; when dreams seemed to die and circumstances overruled. Unlike me, these girls were allowed to stay in school and graduate, but looking from face to face, I didn't see any joy in being here. They weren't forced to attend this classroom, but it gave them a reprieve from embarrassing stares and comments that came from peers and adults alike. I admired their courage to stay in school, but I understood this was a temporary refuge for a few hours out of every day; the real world was just around the corner and couldn't be escaped. These girls were a walking show-and-tell, and the outside world wasn't kind.

I had agonized over today, and now I knew why. Truth sets people free to be who God says they are. I just didn't want it to be my story. *Why me?* I thought. *Please, not now.* My husband and I had taken new jobs and recently moved here with our family. It represented a new beginning; I left my past behind, or so I thought.

Living in a small town, mine was the secret everyone knew but no one talked about, including me. Talking about such things was only airing one's dirty laundry. Most families had a skeleton in the closet, and it was best to keep the door tightly closed. So

I lived in my own prison of shame. I never felt worthy or good enough; no matter how many things I did well or right, I could never shake off this blanket of shame. Its ugly roots had taken hold of my heart years earlier.

Just as nothing could hide their protruding stomachs or mask their hopeless eyes, no disguise was big enough to obscure the transparency of shame. They were young girls, soon to be mothers, and most of them were alone. No words could adequately express the fear or hopelessness within, as well as the rejection they endured from others. It was a hard and difficult road to travel.

Looking at them was like looking in the rearview mirror of my own past; I could see my reflection in their eyes. I thought moving to a new place and having a fresh start would give me a clean slate. I was wrong. I had only moved my emotional baggage to a new place; it was all still there, fully intact. The visual of their reality was like reopening an old scab; my own wounds had never fully healed. Maybe today was for me as well as them.

*How will they know if I don't tell them?* I thought. *I may be the only truth they will hear.*

I wish I could say I was willing; the truth was, I wanted to run as fast as I could. But I chose to stay. I chose to say what they deserved to hear: God's truth. But to do that required complete transparency. Was I ready to give it?

"I know how you feel." The whisper lodged in my throat.

"Yeah, right; sure you do," spewed out as one girl rolled her eyes, locking her arms even tighter across her chest, casting a cold glare on me.

The teacher who invited me nervously shuffled papers; the room filled with an awkward silence. The only sound seemed to be my heart beating. They couldn't endure another pep talk. I did know all too well how they felt.

Carefully choosing my words, tears welling, I whispered the words I so dreaded: "When I was sixteen, I was sitting where you are; I was a teen mom too."

Speaking those words out loud held me captive. Heads lifted, scared eyes searched mine. We connected on the all-too-common ground of teenage pregnancy.

Sharing a common experience can open a door, but only God's love can do the work that has to be done in each heart. I knew these precious girls believed pregnancy defined them, and they had no future; I knew that because I once believed that myself. Possibly no one had told them about unconditional love. Maybe they had never seen the kind of love that renews wounded hearts, heals wrong thinking, and gives life meaning. Only God defines us because He created us, and He planned a way through the messiness of our choices and circumstances. No experience, whether our making or someone else's, can shape or rob our destiny, unless we choose to let it. Although we had connected through teenage pregnancy I was wise enough to know only God's truth could make them truly free.

All eyes were on me.

I talked about my life, where I had been and where I was now. My words were simple and honest; there were moments of tears and times of laughter; comic relief. They relaxed; we bridged the trust barrier. Tension was gone. As I opened my own heart fully, I shared about the kind of hope that gave a pregnant high school dropout a future. When you are in the bottom of the pit, hope is the rope that pulls you out. For me, hope came through the unconditional love of others, who saw past my wrongs and loved me, anyway. Through words of encouragement, investing time and energy, they pointed me toward the promises of a God I didn't know but came to know and to believe. These girls well understood hopeless; they heard, "This is as good as it gets." "Don't expect anything better." "You have no future." They experienced conditional love; for many, it came from abandonment and rejection through a boyfriend, friends, or even family.

*Truth* is a "proven principle," according to *Webster's Dictionary.* For me it was a newfound truth that opened the door for growth, change, and opportunity. I still had healing to do, which I realized that very day, standing in front of those girls. I also became aware that my life might possibly be the first and only picture of not being defined by their circumstances that they had seen and heard, especially the life-changing experience of teenage pregnancy. Through my story, I had the opportunity to help them shift out of where they were into where they could be.

"They don't need a pep talk," God whispered to me that day. "They need you to tell your story."

On what seemed like an ordinary day, I walked into a classroom to give a pep talk. God didn't ask me to change anyone; He just asked me to tell my story.

# CHAPTER 1
## The Way It Was

"She's pregnant," the doctor said as he faced my mother. The meaning of those words did not seem to sink in. I was sixteen.

Mother and I drove home in silence. She drove slower than usual, while I stared out the window, trying to ignore her muffled sobs. In a few hours, my dad would know.

No one spoke during supper. My five-year-old brother didn't understand why things were so quiet. As Mother took him out of the room, I was left to face my dad. He sat at the end of the table, his face buried in his hands. I sat quietly, waiting.

"Is it true?" he finally asked, as his body leaned forward, his face still covered in his hands, never acknowledging my presence.

"Yes," I whispered. A chilling silence filled the room.

His steel blue eyes finally looked into mine. "If I had a gun, I'd shoot you," he said, almost knocking over his chair as he bolted from the room. Paralyzed with fear, I didn't move. He did have a gun, and it was in the next room. I wasn't sure what was going to happen.

Sex wasn't talked about in the 1960s. Whatever it was, it only happened when two people got married. Outside of marriage, it was wrong, and only bad girls did it. Everyone knew who they were; the good girls snubbed them, and the boys bragged about them in the locker room.

Unwed pregnant girls were rare back then. Occasionally, a girl left town for several months. There were rumors, but when she came back—alone—the rumors calmed down, although she was always under suspicion. Even the ones who got married often lived under a cloud of gossip.

I had crossed the line. No one would know or care why; I didn't even know why. I had been considered a nice girl. All of my past accomplishments and my formerly good reputation couldn't stand up under the scrutiny of now being labeled a pregnant, unmarried teenager. In 1966, there was no one to support my parents or me. With no one to tell them differently, they exchanged their hopes and dreams for me for a dark cloud of shame and guilt that would transform their lives, as well as mine, for years to come.

Anger, hurt, and disappointment were just some of the emotions that filled every corner of our small frame house. Days often passed in cold silence; other days were filled with unleashed words of blame. My parents blamed each other, as well as me. The hurt never left my mother's eyes, nor did the guilt leave her voice. She seemed to age prematurely from the worry and anxiety.

Life wouldn't be the same for our family, and I knew I was to blame. I was the one who had made the choice that would change our family forever. Everyone was afraid. Being older and wiser, they were afraid I had no future. They wanted their kids to go to college. Now I couldn't even finish high school. They believed that all my potential died the minute I got pregnant.

A pregnant girl was a wrong example, especially in school, around good kids who might somehow catch it. I was now unmarried, pregnant, and soon to be a dropout. I would never even earn a high school diploma.

Each day became an emotional struggle. No one talked about the future. No one talked to each other, especially not to me. I stayed in my room. During the nights, I cried quietly, going over and over in my mind the events of the past few months. I had so many questions. How did I get to this place in my life? Nothing like this had ever happened in our family. Even though sex wasn't talked about, I knew right from wrong. But during those quiet times in my room, I retraced my life, trying to make sense of why I would make such a wrong choice.

## Looking Back

I could still remember first grade as though it were yesterday. I hadn't been around many kids outside of our family until I started school. We lived in the country, and our only connection to a larger world was through the black-and-white television we got a few months before my sixth birthday. Church on Sunday included the small community of farmers and not many kids my age. I was the baby of three. I watched my older brother and sister get on the yellow bus that took them into town to school, and I couldn't wait till it was my turn. Until that day, my life was rather isolated and non-eventful. Make-believe and fantasyland kept me content.

The first day of school was more than I could have imagined. I had never seen so many kids my age. It didn't take long for the newness to wear off. I began comparing, seeing what they had and what I didn't; what they could do well and what I couldn't do at all. It was a lot like being at home. My older brother and sister were exceptional students, talented, and smart. All I knew how to do was talk, and that had begun to earn me reprimands at school as well as at home. I wanted and needed praise but couldn't seem to measure up in any area. By the age of six, I already had a growing dislike for school. I begged to stay home almost daily with stomachaches. I thought I wasn't smart, and staying home let me hide.

Middle school was more of the same. The principal and I were on a first-name basis, since I visited him in his office weekly.

"Kathy," he said one day, "when you channel that need to talk, you'll do great things. Until then ..."

By the time I entered high school, I longed for a new identity. At last, my brother and sister had graduated, so I didn't have to try to follow in their footsteps anymore. I made passing grades but wasn't outstanding at anything in particular. I certainly didn't stand out in a crowd, except for my height and my teeth. I was taller than both the girls and the boys, which wasn't a good thing. I was labeled "Tree" in middle school, and it followed me to high school. Besides that, there was a noticeable gap between my two front teeth. It had been a source of jokes and ridicule since middle school. "Bet you can outspit anyone. Shame you don't chew." Most of the girls were cute, well dressed, and girly. I was none of those things, but I wanted to be. I didn't know if life held anything for me. I struggled hopelessly with a gnawing insecurity.

The basketball coach was the only one who seemed to see any redeeming value in me. The day I made the basketball team was the highlight of my short-lived life. The day I was cut from the team was the worst public humiliation of my short-lived life. Yes, I was tall. But height and coordination were somehow supposed to be in sync; instead, they were presently colliding. The only thing the coach had to say was, "If your name isn't on the board, then you're not on the team; plain and simple." Then she turned her back and walked away.

Kids can be cruel. That was the longest seven-mile bus ride home, and for once, I wanted to be invisible. I heard all the remarks, even the whispered ones. I sat at the back and made a discovery that day: tears don't make noise.

Mother couldn't fix it, but she wanted to. "You'll be okay," she said. Handing me the keys to Dad's prized 1957 turquoise Chevy Impala, she sent me to the gas station to get a carton of Cokes.

I was a beginner driver. I had driven all over the pasture without hitting one cow. Then I drove the mile down the winding road to church and back quite a few times. Now I was graduating to the small country store on the opposite side of a two-lane highway. Mother wasn't just handing me the keys to the car; she was expanding my horizons. The tears were momentarily exchanged for the thrill of getting my hands on the wheel.

Like so many other things, the thrill was short-lived, as injury was added to insult that day. With the sun shining in my already half-swollen eyes, I failed to see an oncoming car. Not only was Dad's car totaled, but the other driver, an elderly woman, spent the night in the hospital.

Life was unraveling. I continually tasted failure when I longed for success.

For years, I hid my insecurities behind the mask of storytelling and making people laugh, but it became more and more apparent to me that I really wasn't as smart, pretty, or outstanding as my siblings or those around me in school. I believed I was nobody, going nowhere and fast.

Then he noticed me.

On the last day of school, my best friend and I were talking and laughing as we crossed the campus. "Hey, you want to go get a Coca Cola?" We stopped to see two boys in a green Ford Fairlane waiting by the curb. "We're buying," one of them yelled.

I recognized the driver. JJ was a good friend who had a crush on my best friend. As we got closer, I could see the other boy. Being from a small town and a smaller high school, I knew his name was Phil. He never said a word. He just smiled and listened while I talked and made everyone laugh.

As we got out of the car, Phil touched my arm. "Would you like to go out sometime?"

For once, I couldn't speak. No one had ever asked me out. I looked around, thinking he must be talking to someone else.

"I'll call you," he said.

My heart was racing.

He called the next day. "Would you like to go to a movie Friday night?" he asked.

Years later, I would remember what I wore, the movie we saw, and how special I felt. He called that summer again, and again, and again. We were an item. When I was with him, I felt special. We laughed a lot. All my past failures seemed to fade. Finally, someone had chosen me. I was special. Life was good. I didn't realize until much later that I had sought and found acceptance, attention, and love in the smile and in the arms of another kid. That's what we were: two kids.

Just when life was looking up for me, it began to fall apart. Looking for love and wanting acceptance as desperately as I did led me to cross a serious boundary.

I was pregnant.

Months later, he and his parents sat in our small living room. My mother, dad, and I sat across from them, lines drawn. No one smiled. Life had to be handled; decisions had to be made, and soon.

My dad's question hung in the air, waiting for an answer. The same steel blue eyes that pierced through me weeks earlier now locked onto Phil's. It was a man who felt betrayed by his daughter, staring into the kind eyes of a boy who said he loved me. I wondered if he would say the same hateful things to him that he had said to me. Although he only threatened to get his gun and shoot me, any relationship we might have had was emotionally dead. I kept hoping the anger and hurt would subside, but the distance became greater, the emotion colder.

The house grew eerily quiet. I dreaded mealtimes. I got used to the silent treatment; it was the angry outbursts I feared the most. Except for venting his anger, I had become invisible to my father. I never knew which mood would be operating. I didn't want Phil to experience what I had because I was afraid he would change his mind. If he didn't stand with me, then I would be on my own.

Up until that moment, my eyes had been riveted to the floor. Somehow, I was hoping to remain invisible, although I was the center of attention. No one ever asked me what I wanted; I had no voice. But I raised my eyes, hoping beyond hope that his eyes matched his words. Did he want to marry me, or was he doing this out of duty? The one man in my life I thought I could count on wasn't there when I needed him to be; I needed to be able to count on Phil.

Tension filled the room. "Yes sir, I want to marry her," Phil responded, directing both his answer and his eyes to my dad.

Did he really want to marry me? Does any boy want to get married at sixteen? I don't think so. Together, we had made a choice that was beginning to rearrange both our lives and the lives of two families. Sixteen and pregnant; this time, there was no escape into fantasyland. I had crossed the line into a very real world—one I wasn't prepared to live in.

"I want to marry her if she'll have me," he said, and for the first time, our eyes met. I didn't have a clue about the changes that lay ahead, nor did I want to think about them. I only knew he loved me, I loved him, and I would be with someone who made me feel special. My parents didn't share my optimism. They knew what the adult world was really like, and they were afraid to believe that two young kids and a baby, who didn't ask for any of this, would survive.

"She really isn't a bad girl," my mother whispered to Phil's mother. Every head turned to look at me. I looked at the floor. I knew my mother wanted to believe that, but I also knew she didn't. The girl is the one who has to say no. No one had ever told me that, but I knew it anyway. Somehow, this was all my fault.

---

While writing this book, specifically this chapter, I came face to face with what actually happened that night, so many years ago. In my youthful vulnerability and my wounded heart, I took ownership of a belief that would impact every area of my life. It is what we believe about ourselves that guides our attitude, life outlook, decisions, choices, parenting, and relationships.

In *The Purpose Driven Life*, Rick Warren says, "Behind everything you do is a thought. Every behavior is motivated by a belief; every action is prompted by an attitude." In other words, our life is shaped by our thoughts. Sadly, some beliefs are handed down from one generation to another.

That night, as a young girl, I took sole responsibility for hurting and disappointing two families. It was as if my heart and mind became enslaved to shame, guilt, and embarrassment. I not only created the hurt and pain for others, I now carried that burden for life. The only way to survive such heaviness was to prove that somewhere within this awful person was something good. Thus began the endless toiling to prove worth, value, and somehow redemption. For years to come, I would strive to please everyone I came in contact with. Always guiding my motives were these constant thoughts: *Am I good enough? Have I done enough? Do you see me now?*

The good news is that beliefs, even the ones we have held onto and fostered for years, can be changed, exchanged for healthy beliefs. It would be years before I would discover that truth. I will be eternally grateful that God looks at the heart in the person, and He knows how to fix it.

# CHAPTER 2

## For Better or Worse

Little girls play wedding. Like fairy tales, we have visions of castles, a knight on a white horse, and happily ever after. We dream of the day all eyes are on us; the long, white flowing dress, walking on rose petals, adoring eyes, smiling faces, and Kodak memories to remind us that we are, indeed, the vision of our childhood fantasy.

That had been my dream. The reality was two young kids, no friends or family or smiling faces, in a 1962 Plymouth Valiant, trying to fly under the radar before the words "They had to get married" could circulate.

Driving to a nearby city, Phil stopped at the first phone booth and scanned the Yellow Pages in search of a minister. "You're how old?" each one would immediately ask; excuses followed. After several rejections, a minister finally agreed. Phil scribbled down the address, and even though we could not make things right, we could make things legal.

We drove, passing church after church. Ornate architecture, stained glass windows, towering steeples, manicured lawns; they were all pictures of beauty. Our small church back home, nestled unnoticed in the piney woods, paled in such splendor. Winding farther and farther into a rundown, isolated part of the city, we spotted a small building sitting alone at the end of an unpaved road.

Remembering the stark difference in the buildings we passed, I so hoped this wasn't it. Weathered and worn, possibly an army barracks in its earlier years, the addition of a homemade steeple attempted to disguise it as a church. Although my home church didn't compare to the ones we passed, it soared to new heights in contrast to this. My heart sank lower than it already felt; I would always remember my wedding day. This wasn't the memory I wanted.

We both wanted to drive away, but the young minister stood at the door. He didn't say a word, but his eyes said enough. We were kids; over the phone, he couldn't see who he was agreeing to marry. His wife was standing inside the door; the law required a witness. "I need to call your parents," he said to Phil. With that, Phil gave him the home number. We waited; he returned shortly, opened his Bible, and began. With no pomp and circumstance, no wedding dress, no flowers, no loving family surrounding us, two lives unknown by the rest of their world were joined in holy matrimony. He closed his Bible. We thanked him; he nodded. We left; the door closed behind us.

We returned home as Mr. and Mrs.

Our shame had been swept under the legal rug.

The past few months had seemed like an eternity; now the days were speeding by. All too soon, it was time to go—moving to Tennessee, a two-day trip covering sixteen hundred miles. Sandwiched between a new husband and a new father-in-law, with our few worldly possessions and somewhere ahead of us a new life, I kept looking back, straining to see my mother's face as long as I could. Even with the passage of much time, that memory has never faded.

It was one of the coldest Januarys in Texas history. The barren countryside seemed to reflect my thoughts as they wandered back to friends, school, and all I was leaving behind. I knew what I was leaving, but I didn't know what I was facing. The unknown is unsettling at any age, but as a kid whose world had turned upside down, I found it almost impossible to imagine anything good. A whole new life was ahead. Would we make it? Would love hold us together? Frankly, looking back, I didn't even know what love was.

We rode in silence most of the way, with occasional small talk between Phil and his dad. I was the outsider and, now, the unwelcome intruder in the family. No one said that out loud, but actions replaced words of any kind; I felt it. A two-day drive gives you lots of time for thinking. Years earlier, I learned that tears don't make noise, but neither do they make good company. I felt so alone; I would feel that way for many years to come.

"You are entering Tennessee." The world seemed to go from black to white as magical flakes of soft, white snow were falling on the windshield. The winding mountainous roads created a tug of war with the weighed-down station wagon. The old aching fear of more rejection began to creep in. Once again, there seemed to be no place to hide.

The sign read, "Welcome to Kingsport." I hoped I was.

Doubt of ever feeling welcomed anywhere was growing inside. Would I ever be home?

There is a saying, "It's not how you start in life; it is how you finish." I have some additional thoughts that experience has taught me.

We didn't start well; all odds were against us. No one was in our corner; no encouragement, no support. We were all we had, literally. Or so I thought. Through the years, I didn't tell anyone about our wedding day; once again, shame, guilt, embarrassment, and disappointment held me hostage. Those same feelings colored our relationship. Instead of enjoying each other and growing up together, unhealthy barriers grew, dividing my ability to love and be loved. That is what shame does: It keeps us from truth. When I say truth, the core truth at the heart of existence is that God loves us and made us in His image. I did not have that core belief. Too many experiences had distorted my view of me and life in general. The adults who could have helped me see things differently didn't. That is why adults impact how teen parents will emerge from this life-changing experience. Forgiveness, guidance, support, and love bring life and living out of the darkest places of hurt and confusion. Fortunately, there were adults who did come into our lives to help us see God's view and embrace Him. Through their love and guidance, a new core perspective was being birthed in me. In due season, we would emerge as the people God saw when others didn't. Even when we feel and think we are alone, God is always present. He never gives up on us.

We didn't have the wedding of my dreams, but God is full of surprises, and when we least expect it, He exchanges our hurt for His joy. Because of our own journey, I'm passionate about helping others move out of their personal prisons into the light of God's best. We are His workmanship, created for purpose, and designed to love and be loved.

The best is yet to be.

# CHAPTER 3
## The Journey

It had to be a mistake.

"This is it," Phil whispered apologetically. "I'm sorry. Maybe it won't be so bad inside."

No. It was worse.

A narrow sidewalk stood between the small gray cinder block building from the four-lane highway; eighteen wheelers, trucks, and cars blowing past shook the ground under our feet as the noise drowned out everything else. Phil pushed open the door. The stench of stale smoke, the black soot, and the ashes dangling like grotesque spider webs took my breath away. Overwhelmed, speechless, and sixteen hundred miles from home, the tears wouldn't stop. My eyes tried to take it all in, but what little hope I may have had was gone. Phil reached for my hand, but nothing and no one could erase the misery in my heart.

As the dark dust settled, it became apparent that an oversized barrel smothered in black grime, with a large pipe protruding into the ceiling, occupied the center of the small room; this was our heater. Two tiny windows draped with frayed and yellowed plastic curtains filtered in the only sunlight, revealing a thin layer of worn linoleum hidden underneath layers of black gunk. A threadbare sofa, bed, and metal table with chairs made it a "furnished" apartment.

From the church on our wedding day to the remnants of a horror movie, sad went to a new level. My mother's words echoed deep in my heart as things seemed to go from bad to worse. "She's really not a bad girl," her only spoken words that night, months ago in our living room. But by the looks of things, I was. No princess wedding, and the castle had been traded for a dungeon. There was nowhere to run, nowhere to hide, no return trip to normal.

After seeing us settled in our new castle, Phil's father headed home to Texas. This was our home.

For days, we scrubbed and cleaned, but it was a losing battle. Within minutes, more coal dust would settle on everything, so we had to make a choice to either be warm or clean. It was evident we weren't going to have both.

Phil enrolled in the local high school. Riding the bus in the morning and catching a ride with some guys from gym class to his job at the tire recapping shop, he left before daylight and got home after dark.

Days were long and lonely inside those four dingy walls. For the first time in my life, I was completely alone. The isolation was becoming as emotional as it was physical. No television, telephone, or transportation—and no hope. Trips with Phil's aunt to the doctor or walking to the grocery store and laundromat were my only outlets; they offered little relief. The stares and quiet whispers reminded me that I didn't really belong anywhere. (Thirty years later, I heard those same thoughts expressed by the teens I would help; they tagged it "one of those" looks. I learned that some things remained the same.) My body was changing, but my heart and mind were still that of a hurting kid.

As much as I hated the cinder block apartment, it provided a safe refuge from the harsh judgment of the outside world. I wrote letters to friends back home; mostly, I sat and cried. Morning sickness added to the agony. Days dragged by; I grew lonelier.

Then she invaded my life.

It began with church bells ringing one Sunday morning. Church had always been a familiar part of life, and I missed the people in our small community back home. The more isolated I became, the deeper shame covered me like the soot covered our walls. Life in the dungeon was digging its darkness further into my heart.

Sometimes, when circumstances are their worst, we find our courage to do something right, even if we're afraid. I'm pretty sure that is faith, even when we haven't embraced it.

We slipped into a back pew, hoping no one would notice, but one person did notice. Maybe we looked pitiful, huddled in the back row. Maybe she was mission minded or, maybe she was real. Of all the names in the world, her name was Mrs. Blessing (no, really). From her perch on the front row to the back pew where we sat, we had not escaped her gaze. We were trying to leave just as we had come, unnoticed; with long strides and a choir robe flowing in the air, she managed to get between the door and us. She introduced herself and invited us home for Sunday dinner. Actually, she told us we were coming home with them.

From that day on, we became part of their large family. We spent countless hours in that warm, safe kitchen, talking, laughing, and sometimes crying. She listened to my hurts; she gave us love, acceptance, and time. It was like an oasis in the desert.

She treated me like a daughter and Phil like a son, never

seeing either of us as a bad influence on her own three children. She looked past my poor choices and saw the heart inside the girl. Although fairy tales are make-believe, in some ways, I felt like Cinderella: someone had come into my life and showed me unconditional love.

It would be years before I would truly understand the impact of her life on mine. Through her love, acceptance, and time, hope, which was almost dead, revived. It was only a flicker but enough to help me keep on keeping on.

What a difference she made in my young, hurting life.

---

Words, in the form of kindness and encouragement, are powerful enough to heal a wounded heart. When we think we have nothing to give, a smile, a touch, a kind word have more value than gold or silver.

Time is the other gift of equal value. Mrs. Blessing was busy with her own three active children; she was a full-time schoolteacher and a minister's wife. She simply included us in her normal world, where everyone had a place and was made to feel special.

Today, I reap the rewards of her investment, and I pass the gifts she so lovingly gave to me onto others. It's called paying it forward.

"Treat others the way you want to be treated." That is one of the things I learned from Mrs. Blessing.

# CHAPTER 4

## And Baby Makes Three

July came and, with it, the birth of our daughter, Traci.

In the hospital, I was moved to a room with other new mothers. Even though I knew they looked at me as a child with a child, the feelings I had for this baby were anything but childish. All the months of loneliness seemed to dim in comparison to the precious life I held in my arms. She was so tiny and so perfect, a real princess. She was mine, and she was ours. We were a family.

A few months earlier, we had moved to a brown adobe house with a tiny yard, leaving the coal soot and four-lane highway behind. It was farther from the Blessings, but distance was no longer a barrier: We had a car. Phil could drive to school, and he changed job locations to be closer to home. He still left before daylight and returned after dark, but we were in a small neighborhood surrounded with grandmas. God knew I was going to need every single one of them.

One of the grandmas lived next door. Her name was Mrs. Scott. For weeks, she kept a running list of what a baby would need, adding something else almost daily. Bottles, diapers, blankets, gowns; the list kept growing. We didn't have a clue what babies needed. While I was still in the hospital, she handed Phil the list, and he went shopping where she directed. We didn't have much money, but he had been saving all he could from his part-time job at the gas station. Visiting hours were strict, allowing him to only stay for one hour each night. He would come straight from work, covered in oil and grease, and stand and stare at the tiny baby in the nursery that had his last name. He was a proud dad.

I had no idea how hard being sixteen and having a small baby would be.

The demands from a baby are overwhelming at any age, but it's very frustrating, trying to think like an adult when your maturity and experience level still function as a kid.

To make matters worse, from the time we brought her home, Traci screamed and cried. This went on for weeks. When we took her to the doctor, the pediatrician said, "This baby has something really wrong." I panicked, but Phil remained calm. She was admitted back into the hospital.

We were put in a room with a baby who had cerebral palsy and several other abnormalities. The mother was in her forties and had several older children at home to care for. She was exhausted from no sleep, and her little girl needed constant holding. While Traci slept, I held the other baby and let that mother get some rest. I would rock this baby, who wiggled, slipped, and slid in my arms. She would toss her head to look at me and grin. She was precious, but the joy she brought would only be for a short time. Each day, the doctors added to an already bleak prognosis, and that mother faced the reality that her little girl would never go home.

Traci was allergic to milk. Within days, we were going home with a healthy baby who needed a strange kind of milk. But I couldn't erase the faces of the children who would never leave and who would never be healthy or normal. I had never experienced the sights and sounds of a children's hospital, and I'll never forget it. I may have been only sixteen, but I had a healthy baby. I couldn't imagine what they were going through.

The pharmacy had to order the milk, and not only was it expensive, it only came in powder form. The formula had to be mixed with an electric mixer, and I didn't have one. The next best thing was a rotary eggbeater, but the powder would gum up in huge clumps. Even a patient grandma would have been frustrated. I struggled to time things right, and the bottles would be too hot. I would pour expensive formula down the drain and start over. Every day found me collapsed in a sea of tears at the kitchen table, while the sounds of a screaming baby echoed throughout the house. When she slept, I did laundry, fixed formula, and cried, and not always in that order. I was exhausted, and crying was intermingled with everything.

It wasn't any better for Phil. He had the responsibility of being a husband, dad, provider, and student. He slipped and slid through the snow and ice to school, to his job at the gas station, and home after dark to do homework. Every night, he came in the back door covered in oil and grease, too tired to even eat. His job paid minimum wage, and with rent, doctor bills, formula, groceries, and other stuff, there was no light at the end of a very dark tunnel. The weight and responsibility of a family sat on his young shoulders.

Our only joy centered on a tiny baby girl. As she grew, we watched every move she made. There were so many times I wished she had come when I was older and could have enjoyed the life that comes from doing things in the right order.

I longed to be a teenager again. I missed being with kids my age, doing what normal teens do. I had no dreams anymore; the four walls of our tiny house began to feel like a prison. I couldn't see past the present circumstances, and no bright future even remotely existed in my mind.

This seemed to be as good as it would ever get.

———————————

I was sixteen; I have worked with teens who are younger and are raising a child. It is hard to put into words a child parenting another child. But it can be done and successfully. I'm proof of that, and through the years, I've known hundreds of other teens who successfully parented children. I have also had the opportunity to work with teens who placed their children into the loving arms of others. Both options are emotionally and physically difficult and require grave sacrifice. Just as becoming a pregnant teen began with a choice, there are many other choices you will face during this season of life. The one thing I will say for certain is this: A teen cannot do this alone; end of discussion. There has to be mature, loving, caring adults coming alongside. I had my faith, Phil, and loving adults. It took all of us.

# CHAPTER 5

## Going Home

Phil graduated from high school in December. We both wanted to go back to Texas and wondered why we had moved to Tennessee in the first place. In that era, most girls who got pregnant went away, gave their baby up for adoption, and returned home, hoping to live as though nothing had happened. Even as I write this, after all these years, I'm not sure why we went away. We had gotten married. True, Phil's uncle had offered a job, but he probably could have gotten a job in our hometown.

This is what I do know: Mrs. Blessing and Mrs. Scott were divinely placed at the right time.

The likelihood of two sixteen-year-olds surviving the kind of year we experienced is rare. Some would have said we didn't stand a chance, and if those two ladies hadn't been there, we might not have. Although marriage was supposed to somehow right a wrong, a legal document doesn't carry much clout in day-to-day reality, especially when you are a kid yourself and still think like a kid. We needed encouragement, wise counsel, and guidance. When they came into our lives, we were two scared kids; they embraced us in their hearts, loving us unconditionally. They took time to care and get involved, and that made all the difference. Possibly because of their influence, Phil, Traci, and I remained a family.

This time, we were Texas bound. Once again, I returned to fantasyland, thinking that if we went home, we could pick up where we left off. The old station wagon that had taken us away a year ago was now taking us back.

Time stands still for no one. We were teenagers who were also parents. Our normal was different. Other kids our age were doing different things. They couldn't relate to us; we didn't relate to them. Age was the only common factor, while lifestyle and responsibilities were as far as the east is from the west. We didn't fit anymore.

We didn't know then that our dreams didn't have to die just because we were raising a child. Phil had his high school diploma, but he knew he needed to go to college. Growing up, he thought he'd enter the medical field, maybe become a dentist. College seemed a big reach, let alone dental school, so he traded his dreams for something more realistic. East Texas Baptist in Marshall was the closest four-year college. We drove over, looked around, signed a student loan, borrowed a pickup truck, and headed to our new home.

This time I was ready.

In many ways, the dungeon in Tennessee had prepared us for married housing. It was a one-bedroom duplex, with the kitchen, dining room, and living room as one room. It gave new meaning to the term close quarters. There were no secrets from the neighbors; walls were tissue paper thin. One morning, one of the neighbors closed her kitchen window, and it fell out onto the ground below. Although the duplex was very old, it was clean.

The one thing we all had in common was our youth. Some were struggling to pay for school and survive. We fell into that category. Others were taking their time and becoming professional students. Phil worked for the school, painting dorm rooms, driving a bus in the winter, and doing odd jobs for pay.

I needed a job, but I was a seventeen-year-old dropout. Even then, a high school diploma was valuable. Woolworth's Department Store hired me to stock shelves and clean the grill after lunch. I worked from early till late, making minimum wage, which at that time was around seventy-five cents. I worked six days a week, leaving Traci with a lady who kept children in her home. I barely made enough to buy groceries.

After working at Woolworth's for several months, a neighbor told me about a job opening at Joe Weisman's Department Store, a well-known Texas landmark among the southern elite. With his brother Martin, Joe Hirsch was co-owner of this old established family business. I interviewed with Joe. I didn't have a resume; I didn't even know what one was. I was seventeen, had less than a tenth grade education, and had a lot of emotional baggage. Self-worth was low on my attributes. Guilt and shame kept me buried in layers of fear: fear of failure, fear of not being good enough, fear that life held nothing for me. Although I could still make people laugh and think I was this great outgoing person, I kept everyone at arm's length. If anyone got too close, they might see the real me.

Although I was scared, I was even more desperate. We needed a paycheck, and my fingers and hands were rubbed raw from scrubbing the grill at Woolworth's. I didn't know how to dress for success, and I didn't know the first thing about interviewing skills. All I knew was that I needed a good job, and I knew it paid more than the one I had. For the first time in my life, real determination to make a change rose up in me.

"Have you ever worked a switchboard?" Joe asked.

"No sir," I said, "but I can."

"Can you gift wrap?" he asked.

"I help my mother at Christmas," I replied. "They say my packages look better than all the others." No one had ever said that, but I was determined and desperate.

"You are really young," he said. "I'm not used to hiring anyone this young. You didn't graduate from high school; you don't have a diploma. I value education."

I sat quietly. He was only saying what I knew to be true; I was a young high school dropout.

"I really need this job, Mr. Hirsch. I won't disappoint you, I promise."

Two weeks passed. During that time, I called every other day to ask Joe if he'd decided. My sheer determination either won him over or wore him out, but I got the job. I may have been the first seventeen-year-old dropout he had ever hired.

I kept my promise. It's easy to do a good job and give 100 percent when you love where you work, the people you work with, and the people you work for. I learned so much during that time. I learned what a positive environment and positive people do for a person with low self-esteem. We were treated like we were members of a special family. Sometimes, that included a reprimand, but it was always followed by something positive. We were valued first as people and then as employees. I learned what a healthy work environment should be.

I learned to operate a complicated switchboard and wrap packages as well as anyone; through those seemingly minor accomplishments, I gained confidence. But the people I worked with saw even more in me than I saw in myself.

"You need to finish school," they often encouraged.

At home, Phil said the same thing. But I was scared of more failure. I couldn't return to high school, and even if I could, I didn't want to. I didn't want to be a nineteen-year-old in the tenth grade.

Then Phil heard about the general equivalency diploma (GED). It involved taking a three-part test over a period of three days. If I passed, I would have a high school diploma. If I failed, I would be embarrassed, and the tests included many things I didn't know. Although I had spent plenty of time in the school of hard knocks, my academic education ended after the first semester of the tenth grade. Real life hadn't included geometry, chemistry, or literature. Fear said, "If you don't try, you won't fail again." But another thought quietly said, *What if you pass?*

I said that over and over: *What if I pass?* I had no idea where that thought came from, but I knew I would have one less strike against my name if I passed. I would no longer be a high school dropout. We paid the fee, and I spent three grueling days, taking tests on subjects that were as foreign to me as Greek. Then I waited.

Weeks passed slowly. Every day at work, someone would ask if I'd heard back from my test. I really believed that I would have to tell everyone I had failed. With my limited educational background, I knew there was no conceivable way I could pass. It would make no sense if I did.

The envelope arrived on a Saturday. At least I would have time to deal with the disappointment before facing them at work. I could hardly open it; I felt sick.

Phil's patience and my procrastination collided. "Just open it," he finally said.

I slowly opened the envelope, but I couldn't understand it.

Phil took it and began to scan it with his eyes. Slowly, a grin spread across his face.

"You passed all three parts," he said. "You passed the GED. You are a high school graduate."

I stood there, staring at the piece of paper, with Traci locking her small arms around my legs.

When you've spent most of your youth losing, failing while watching others succeed and win and be chosen, at some point along the way, you begin to believe that you are a failure, a loser, and not as smart or talented as others. Maybe you don't go around saying, "I'm a failure" or "I'm a loser," out loud, but down deep in the secret place of your heart, those thoughts take root and grow. When circumstances continually reinforce that belief, the lie grows. Without realizing it, you may begin to live out that lie. That's where I was. I even thought they made a mistake and another envelope would come, saying the first one was in error.

But it was true. It took me several days to believe I passed one of the most difficult things I had ever attempted. I called my parents first.

Why was that so important? I wanted my parents to be proud of me; I'm pretty sure that most kids want that.

People who lived in the country were on a party line, which meant they shared phone privileges with their neighbors. Phone calls usually had a purpose, and there were no long conversations. Plus long-distance calls were charged by the minute and expensive on a shoestring budget.

Mother answered the phone. "Mom, I have something to tell you and Dad." Silence. "I have some really good news." More silence. "I passed the GED. I graduated from high school."

There was a sigh. "Ah, did you really?" she said.

"Will you tell Dad when he comes in?"

"I sure will," Mother said. "I'm proud of you."

"I'm proud of you." It was the first time I had heard those words. A few days later, we drove to their house to show them my GED certificate and scores. Dad looked it over and handed it to Mother. They both smiled and congratulated me for pursuing my education. Dad just kept staring at the piece of paper.

---

I want to connect the past to the present for greater understanding.

My parents were part of the Great Depression generation. Dreams didn't guide their lives; hard work and survival did. Mother grew up in a sharecroppers' family, which meant moving around, living in poverty, and sometimes not knowing where the next meal would come from. Dad was the baby of eleven kids. His parents were older when he was born, and his brothers and sisters raised him. Although he was an incredible athlete, no one in his family saw him play football. Mother kept newspaper clippings that were tattered and yellowed with age; that was all that remained of another time and possibly unfulfilled dreams. Both he and Mother had an incredible work ethic and strong moral character. I wouldn't trade what they taught me. Sometimes, their method of communicating could have used some softer tactics, but warm and fuzzy weren't part of who they were. They were good people who had survived more than our generation will ever understand.

My parents valued education, and they both understood it was a privilege, and for them, it once was a dream. Mother didn't graduate; she lacked one year. Dad graduated and earned a full ride to the University of Texas to play football. Instead, he married his high school sweetheart and joined the army to serve his country in World War II. After the war, he found a job in the oilfields to support a growing family and never pursued his education. They both had lost dreams and wanted us to do better.

I think this is true of most parents. Deep within is a hope that their children will accomplish more and leave an even greater mark. I know I want that for my children and grandchildren.

Mother and Dad didn't throw a party; there were no fireworks, but I knew they were proud of me. I think, possibly, that was the glimmer of hope there were still good things to come; that teenage pregnancy didn't define or limit my life.

I couldn't change a lot of things about my life, but I had changed one thing: I was no longer a high school dropout. At the age of nineteen, I had tasted success. It was a good feeling, one I decided I wanted to enjoy more often.

# CHAPTER 6

## One Step Forward, Two Steps Back

What is success? How do you measure it?

I had passed the GED. Now what? I almost stopped there. When the excitement of the moment wore off, the old mind-set began to play the same song, with endless verses. I thought I was just lucky, not smart. I had invested years believing I wasn't as smart or as capable as others; that didn't suddenly disappear because of one test.

Phil was moving forward and would have a college degree. In my mind, I still saw myself as a high school dropout and the girl who had to get married. To me, the differences were becoming glaringly obvious. What if Phil outgrew me intellectually? What if he decided he wanted someone smarter, prettier, and with a career? My GED did give me a taste of accomplishment, but it didn't erase years of wrong thinking. I defined myself by what I couldn't do instead of what I could do.

However, sometimes even misguided beliefs can propel us onto a right road. As defeating and limiting as those beliefs, they drove me to enroll in night school; I signed up to take a typing class.

I went to three classes and withdrew. It was advanced typing, and I was a beginner. I quit before I could fail. So I signed up for a different class, in shorthand. Any woman who could type and do shorthand could get a good job.

After five classes, I dropped out. The pattern was looking very familiar.

More defeats only seemed to reinforce the fact that I was not smart or that I couldn't complete what I had started. No one told me those courses might not be right for me, that perhaps I had other talents. Instead, I just thought I wasn't a fit for college.

Phil graduated and got a job in our hometown, and we moved into a small garage apartment across from the city park, where four-year-old Traci and I played on the swings and had picnic lunches. Occasionally, someone who didn't know us thought I was babysitting my younger sister; I didn't tell them otherwise.

Moving back to our hometown wasn't easy. Sticks and stones may break bones, but hurtful looks and whispered gossip can hurt more. The four walls of our apartment felt safe; lonely, but safe.

Phil wanted to go to church. I did not.

I did not want any part of church. I knew I didn't fit with any age group, and I didn't fit in with church in general. How could I believe in a God I couldn't see who supposedly loved me when I often felt so rejected by the people closest to me? I longed for acceptance yet believed it would never come. I struggled with overwhelming shame. I had no peace and no joy. I thought my life was the problem, but the problem was within me.

I had no answers to my pain, but help was on the way.

It began as a gentle whisper: "The choice is yours."

It was two in the morning; I thought I was dreaming. Tears flowed onto the pillow; I was jolted awake. Was it a dream? Was I seeing things? It had been hours of the usual tossing and turning, and little sleep.

The wall became a movie screen, and a silhouette of a cross was outlined. *It has to be a dream,* I thought, yet there was no fear, no panic—and still no sleep. My eyes were fixated on the images in front of me and the object that seemed to be staring back at me. Why was I crying? I realized the tears that caused me to awake were still streaming down my face. I didn't want to move; nothing made sense, but I longed to remain in this moment. The silhouette was captivating.

*The choice is yours,* seemed to penetrate my thoughts.

"What choice?" This conversation was within me, yet I had no idea who I was talking to.

Phil was sleeping soundly as I eased out of bed. I had heard plenty through the years about a cross, a God in heaven, and the Son of God everyone called Jesus. But it meant nothing to me personally. Mrs. Blessing and Mrs. Scott had both introduced me to unconditional love, but others who professed being Christian had not. My heart was fragile, and words of kindness and love were rare; I felt inadequate to measure up to Christian standards, although I was no longer sure what those looked like. I knew I could never become one of them, a Christian, because I wasn't good enough. Over time, I wasn't sure I even wanted to believe in their God if He was like most of them.

But that night, something was different. "What do I do?" I whispered into the darkness. There was no answer; just a gnawing thought that repeated over and over. *The choice is yours.* What choice? I had to talk to someone who understood. Right now.

I couldn't wait until morning. Hunting clothes in the dark, I dialed the pastor of the church Phil had dragged me to, got in the car, easing the door shut so as not to wake anyone, and drove across town to their home.

The pastor and his wife stood under the porch light, waiting for me. It was 2:30 in the morning, yet they both seemed excited to see me. The three of us talked candidly. More poured out than I planned: the hurt, the rejection, feelings of never being good enough.

The pastor hung his head. "I'm so sorry that people have hurt you; that's not Jesus," he added. Then he told me about his Jesus, the one Mrs. Blessing and Mrs. Scott had showed me. That night, I made another life-changing decision, one that would change my life as I knew it.

In the early hours of the morning, as the sun was just coming up, I returned home. Phil was still asleep; I sat down at the kitchen table to contemplate the past few hours. Of my own free will, I had taken a step of faith and asked God to come into my life. In my mind, the amazing part was He had accepted that invitation from someone as imperfect as me.

I couldn't explain what had happened. By the looks of things, nothing had changed. Unpaid bills lay on the table. I was a young girl who became a mother too young, and I still had lots of fears to overcome, but for the first time, I had peace in spite of the circumstances of life.

Looking back, I see the Lord during that time in Tennessee. He was there in the love of Mrs. Blessing; He was there in the guidance of Mrs. Scott. He was there hours earlier, when I asked Him into my heart.

And He was there in the knock on my door.

# CHAPTER 7

## I Can See Clearly Now

"I was out walking and thought I'd stop by," she said, grinning.

I had first met Leta Fae when I grudgingly went to church with Phil. During the week, she taught English at the small college in our town. On Sunday, she traded in her professor hat to talk about her first love, Jesus. I had never heard anyone talk about God with such excitement. With every word, He came alive. Up until that point, my view of God was the Man upstairs, waiting for us when we die. She didn't talk about how much better life was going to be in heaven; she explained the power of a living God. Her perspective was almost contagious. I wanted to believe what she said, but something in the back of my mind kept whispering, "What if she's wrong?"

The timing of her entrance into my life a year earlier had been perfect.

This English professor at the junior college began by asking me about goals and dreams. No one had ever asked me that. "I want you to take my class," she would say. "Just one class; trust me. You'll enjoy it."

I made excuses, dodging her at every turn, but in the end, I went. Just like her Bible class, I hung on every word she said. I had forgotten that the one subject I excelled in school was English; by the end of that semester, my confidence was flourishing, and I signed up for another.

After I passed the GED, I had tasted the sweet flavor of success. Now I had tasted it again. I began to take more classes, with each success adding confidence. Slowly, I was completing the basic courses toward an associate degree, but one class stood in the way: speech. I've since read that the greatest fear next to the fear of death is speaking in public. I was terrified; what I didn't know was, so was everyone else. On the day of my first speech, I literally threw up (fortunately, before I got to class).

This was my largest class, and I was the oldest student. I worked for weeks compacting seven written pages into a four-minute speech. After I muddled through my patriotic "yellow ribbon round the oak tree" speech, a six-foot-five basketball player proceeded to tell this class of college students how to tie shoelaces in double knots. After wrapping his lanky body over the podium, stammering and stuttering his way through a minute and a half presentation, he made a 97, and I made a 95. On the way out the door, I deposited my seven-page speech in the trashcan. That young athlete helped me see the light: don't take that class so seriously. From that day on, I thought up speeches in the car sitting in the parking lot. I made an A for the course, but more importantly, I enjoyed it.

Fear didn't win.

So it was no surprise that Leta Fae was the one who came to my door within hours of my spiritual experience. She was on her usual walk; I was reflecting on things, wondering where I went from here. As I shared my heart, the wonder of this new life, she opened the pages of a very worn and tattered Bible. As she read, words seemed to come alive and leap off the pages. I not only understood them; they slid through my ears into a waiting and willing heart. A warm peace, like the one I had experienced hours earlier, embraced me. Tears began to fall from my eyes, just as they had during the night. I knew this was real; it was indeed a new day.

Life is hard when you do it your way. Without Jesus, hope and peace are only illusions; faith is nonexistent. It's hard to believe in a God you can't see, when many of the ones who wear His name have themselves misunderstood who He is. The one I met birthed His presence into my heart; I would come to understand the power of relationship over religion. That changes everything from the inside out.

But old habits die hard. Often when someone becomes a Christian, we mistakenly think they will be new: new thinking, new attitude, and new person. When Christ is invited in, it is a new birth, a new beginning, but with the same body. Transformation is often confused with "microwave thinking." One is an ongoing process; the other is a quick fix.

God begins to shine His light into the hidden places of our heart and mind, and sometimes, we don't even understand how deeply rooted some things are, but He does. Only He can clear away the debris of wrong thinking to open the path to a better way. Self-help books, feel-good words, and standing in front of a mirror repeating, "I like myself, I like myself," can't cut through years of scars from confusing words or hurtful circumstances. Guilt and shame, like so many other emotional parasites, are birthed in the vulnerability of a wounded heart and become the gifts that literally keep on giving. You could say they have a shelf life of forever. In some families, they are handed down to the next generation to do unto them what they had accomplished with the previous group. Some people have even wondered if guilt and shame are genetic because the pattern of devastation becomes so obvious within families. Inviting Jesus Christ into your heart changes the equation. He changes what we can't.

Asking Him into my life was a strategic right turn; it changed the possibility for everything, including releasing the power of the past. At that point, I began a new journey of growing and changing. It was (and is) a slow process. God is loving and kind; He doesn't give us more than we are ready to receive. I came to realize there have always been people throughout my life who seemed to help me focus onward and upward. They were there in the darkest times in Tennessee. They were there when I came home. Now I know it was a loving God, loving me through them.

# CHAPTER 8

## Finding Your Dream and Setting a Goal

Life was changing; daily, I experienced a peace and joy that reminded me I wasn't alone and never had been. Someone said it's like getting glasses for the first time. You didn't know you couldn't see until you put them on. Suddenly, your world is open to more than you can take in quickly. That's what life was like; each day, throughout the day, life became an adventure of seeing differently. I was finally free to be the real me, not the person I thought I was through the eyes and opinions of others.

I was taking steps, baby steps, but at least I was moving forward. The English class led to another class. What I didn't know was Leta Fae was talking to her colleagues, asking them to encourage me to take their classes. I felt so special as various professors asked me to take different classes. With each step of faith, I had to face my fear of thinking I wasn't smart enough; however, there was a stronger voice reminding me, *You can do it.*

Fourteen years at a junior college; in the beginning, I was embarrassed that a normal two-year program had been stretched into fourteen years. But a fellow teacher changed that perspective:

"Not many people would have persevered that long; you aren't a quitter on anything, including people."

Her words would become prophetic.

Growing up, I was called "Chatty Kathy"; people said I had been vaccinated with a phonograph needle. From first grade on, every trip I made to the principal's office was for talking. No one saw it as a gift.

Now I was going to major in speech. Life does give us a twist sometimes.

I never stopped going to school. In 1985, I reached my goal.

I completed the last two years at the University of Texas at Tyler. At last, I wasn't the oldest student. Most of the others were my age and serious about education. Many of them had been emotionally beat up through the school of real life. For some, dreams had died; for others, needs had changed; and for everyone, youth was gone. No one had time or energy to waste. We all wanted to find our special area of talent, learn how to utilize what potential we had, and find our practical place in an ever-changing world.

God had given me the gift of talking. In childhood, it was seen as a weakness. Growing up, I was the class clown, the life of the party, the person who covered insecurity through the gift of gab. Now, I was learning it was also my strength. In college, I discovered that people listened to what I had to say. They were genuinely interested, and I felt valued. I didn't have to entertain to win acceptance or approval.

One day, my speech professor asked me to stop by his office. "What do you plan to do after you graduate?" he asked.

I said I didn't know.

"People listen to you," he continued. "You're real and refreshing. You have a lot of heart. Have you ever considered social work?"

I wasn't sure what social work involved, but I had a heart for people who were down and out. I always seemed to be encouraging others, the eternal optimist, always seeing the good as well as the potential in other people.

Leta Fae had asked me years earlier about goals. Her encouragement had put me on the road to college. Now my speech professor was telling me I had a purpose.

Ever since God had entered my life, each day was like a journey that was leading toward a greater plan. College had changed me intellectually, but faith was transforming my life.

During those years of going to school, life was going on. We had two more children, more responsibilities, and normal day-to-day stuff. A normal day for any family is hectic and chaotic, but a dream had been planted into my mind, and it remained solid in my heart. As much as I wanted to lay it down, I couldn't. At first, it had been the voices from others who believed for me, until I could believe for myself. The day came when I realized I believed; it was my dream.

There had been so many people sprinkled throughout my journey to say the right words at just the right time. Words, their words, were opening a new way of thinking, seeing, and becoming the person I was meant to be.

In August 1985, at the age of thirty-five, I became a college graduate. As I walked across the stage in that auditorium, the air was thick with excitement and applause. Many of us couldn't have done this without the love and support of family. This was truly a shared experience and one witnessed by people of all ages. We weren't just graduates; we were moms, dads, aunts, uncles, brothers, sisters, and in some cases grandparents. It was a tribute to tenacity, hard work, and a belief that we had a valued place in society. We were raising the bar and demonstrating that expectations come with a higher price for some of us. Although there is no doubt that each person who walked across that stage that night wanted, at some point in the journey, to quit as others had, that was a moment worth the price.

Five years later, at the age of forty, I would complete a master's degree.

# CHAPTER 9

## A New Season

Just as one chapter closes, another opens. Life is about the journey, including the detours made from our choices, the choices of others, or unforeseen events. All these things play a major role leading to and fulfilling our divine purpose and destiny, even when it doesn't make sense. We get to choose the outcome. I was learning to raise the bar of expectations, while allowing joy and success to override fear and failure.

In the fall of 1986, Phil and I made another life-changing decision. It required leaving our now comfortable life and moving to a much larger area. Traci was a freshman in college; our other two children were in high school. This was the only home they had known. It was probably one of the hardest decisions we would ever make, yet years later, we would see the bigger picture.

The day we drove away in the moving van, I kept looking back. We had covered a lot of territory and done a lot of living since our humble beginning in Tennessee. In some ways, I still felt like that young, scared girl saying goodbye to the only life she knew. Our worldly possessions had grown from being packed into a 1963 station wagon to a twenty-two-foot U-Haul truck. The one thing that remained the same was the unknown. This time, as strange as it seemed, we both knew God was in this.

In some ways, it was a new beginning. Phil was expanding from building houses in a small town to building schools in an urban school district. The kids settled into a new high school, making new friends, in a city atmosphere. I was finding my way around in unfamiliar territory.

I had fulfilled my dream; I was a college graduate. As passionate as I once was about a college degree, there had never been a plan past that. No goal; no career; just to say I did it. Many times along the way, when I became discouraged, there was always an inner prodding that wouldn't let me quit. "You can do it," I would repeat often. The day I walked across that stage was more than a dream finally lived. I proved that life doesn't stop because of wrong choices. Circumstances can't hold us when we choose to believe in what we can do, instead of what we can't do, and work extremely hard. I hadn't done any of it alone. No one is an island. I had been blessed with lots of supportive, loving people.

Now I didn't know if there was a next step.

Then God stepped in.

While I was thinking my purpose was complete, God had a much larger picture of me and His purpose.

We plan our ways; God orders our steps. While I was growing in confidence through the years, earning a college diploma, I had no idea those steps would open doors to a plan and purpose beyond my limited thinking.

In 1987, I became a counselor for a new program targeting teens who were at risk of dropping out of school. In fact, they made up the highest number of dropouts in Texas. The one thing these students had in common was they were either pregnant or had had a baby.

It was a new era, and lawmakers were finally seeing the importance of education for all students. There was no more, "One strike and you're out," like I had experienced in the 1960s. I felt the old passion return that had motivated me to work hard for a degree. I made it to the other side of teen pregnancy and wanted to extend that possibility to others.

The room was packed the day of our first support group meeting. Memories were still fresh on my mind from the day, only weeks earlier, that I first shared my own story with a small group of young girls who attended the off-campus pregnancy school. This day would be similar, yet different. Girls and guys alike were waiting to see what this was all about. Most of them came to school when they could, blended in with normal students, and certainly didn't want to be singled out. They had been encouraged by the school counselors to come to this support group meeting. Many weren't too happy to be there. Their faces embodied their lack of interest and skepticism.

What they didn't know was that I, too, was scared. I was still new to this openness. My secret had been locked away for so long that even though the door to truth and freedom was finally open, it still felt strange. Secrets literally begin to define us, to become our truth. I was still shedding my old thinking as each day allowed me to enjoy this newfound freedom. I felt like a captive being set free. Now I was stepping into a new arena to help others.

To say I felt inadequate wouldn't cover it. I knew this was more than a job; it was a ministry, and I knew God had led me to this point in my life. In 1966, I was a teenage mother and school dropout. While I had focused on overcoming my past, it was the past that became credentials for the present.

No one cares how much you know, until they know how much you care.

They stared at me; I looked from face to face, slowly taking in all the ages, unspoken questions, and mixed emotions. The atmosphere was charged with indifference and impatience.

"Why are we here?" a boy demanded.

"You are all teen parents or soon to be teen parents," I calmly replied. "I'm here to help you help yourselves."

Eyes rolled and bodies shifted, as each one became even more guarded. I had been on the receiving end of this before and understood their distrust. I continued, "You represent the highest dropout rate in the state, and we want you to stay in school and graduate." Being a guy, he accepted the logic. Boys don't want "touchy feely" anything.

I told them my title, gave them an overview of the ways I could help them, and explained that we would have weekly meetings and discuss whatever topics and issues they struggled with. "No one has to come," I stated, "but this is your forum. This is where you can vent, learn from each other, and find ways to cope with the problems you face. This won't be a gripe session, but it will be a safe place for you to grow and heal."

I continued, "We need to get to know each other. And you need to know one more thing: what is discussed here stays here. Some people say time heals all things; I've learned talking about things is the best healer, but we have to feel safe to do that. Nothing leaves this room."

The room was now quiet.

Names and ages were reluctantly shared. Then a question came from the left side of the lecture room: "Why did you want this job? Most teachers don't think we'll make it very far. Do you feel that way?"

The young girl was curious yet bold, as all eyes followed her words directly to me. I stood in the center of the school lecture room, which normally seated around a hundred students. It was probably two-thirds full. Just gazing at so many of them was overwhelming. I didn't just feel small; I felt like David standing before Goliath. I remembered how alone I felt in my struggles at sixteen, and yet to see so many sharing this experience at such young ages was a revelation even I struggled to grasp. It was going to take more than a slingshot to bring down the problems in this room.

I had prayed earlier that day and asked the Lord to walk me through that meeting. I had also asked Him to make it clear as to what I was to say and not say. They deserved to live the life God had always planned for each one of them, but without truth and wisdom, they would remain locked in their circumstances and possibly miss the life they could still have. Hope had to be planted, and it would take honesty and transparency to grow.

Like the day in that classroom with that small handful of young girls, I felt my new truth travel up my throat as I heard the words softly escape through my lips. "I know how you feel. I understand many of your battles; I've been where you are. I was a teen mother when I was sixteen." I recognized the familiar gasp. Some were speechless; others looked from face to face with suspicion and disbelief.

I boldly continued, "I'm here because I believe in you. There was a time no one believed in me, and then people came into my life who did. Those people made a huge difference, and through their words and actions, they gave me a new picture of myself. Over time, I came to understand: I didn't have to be defined by my circumstances. But it took lots of hard, hard, hard work. I was worth the effort. And so are you."

The ice was broken, and amazingly, I was still standing. It had been an intense few minutes.

That was the beginning. The ensuing weeks brought lively and often heated discussion as the conversation became more relaxed, open, and honest. Some of the students didn't come back; however, new students began to surface. Word spread that this was a safe place. As the numbers grew, I was amazed there were so many.

While some people attempt to place blame on the entertainment industry as to why unwed pregnancy occurs, the real culprit can be found in unmet emotional needs. But the age-old adage, "looking for love," still wins out. Unmet emotional needs will always have the greatest influence: "He said he loved me; I felt important; someone chose me."

Different needs, different experiences, but same outcome. Each week, these kids filled a lecture room and talked about their new reality as a parent. Life had drastically changed. If there was hope before, it was gone, and a bleak present remained.

While the boys didn't face the shame of a protruding stomach, the girls gave new meaning to "show and tell." Girls didn't fit into their clothes, with their friends, or into the mainstream of school. Both the boys and girls experienced a shattering of hopes and dreams for their futures. Some took ownership of their responsibilities, but sadly, the majority walked away from theirs.

Their problems were overwhelming. Grades, school attendance and graduation couldn't compete with jobs, childcare, health care, the cost of living, and often the war zone on the home front. Their external problems were overwhelming. Some had places to live; others didn't. They faced battles with teachers at school, employers on the job, and parents at home. They were paying a huge price for a poor choice, and many were choosing to drop out of school.

I took that personally. Often in life, we don't know what we have until we lose it. This is true of education. It is a privilege; it is not a right. These kids now had both the right and the privilege I once was denied. They could go attend class with the opportunity to earn a high school diploma. As a society, we have come a long way in valuing education for all people. Yet the obstacles they faced were bigger than their perceived need for a diploma. They were fighting adult problems, with only a child's resources.

Without loving, mature people in their lives, they couldn't make it, nor could the cycle of teen pregnancy be broken in their future generations. They needed all of us to surround them, support them, and help them in whatever ways we could. Parents have the greatest influence and opportunity to help their children navigate through this part of their lives. Sadly, many of these kids did not have this. As their stories unfolded, I found myself in a position of being educated on all sides of the issue.

# CHAPTER 10

## In the Courtroom of Public Opinion

"They think getting pregnant is glamorous." That thought never entered my own mind, and throughout all the support group discussions, that statement had never surfaced, yet it was voiced in the teacher's lounge.

"Have you always been naïve?" a teacher asked. "Those kids got in this mess because they wanted to. They knew what they were doing. Jobs like yours just condone and encourage what they do."

"How do you work with those kinds of kids?" I was all too often asked. "They deserved what they got. We shouldn't reward them. That's all your job does."

Too often, the battles were fought with the very ones who were supposed to educate, not judge or condemn. Few seemed to care why or how kids had gotten to this place. There seemed to be two extremes of thinking: Some were angry at them, while some pitied them as failures. Both extremes damaged, just like the extreme messages that have confused us all. Too often, it appeared that many adults weren't angry that kids were having sex; the anger seemed to be directed at them for getting caught.

"If they're going to do it," one person stated, "they could at least be responsible. Taxpayers like me are tired of supporting irresponsibility."

I understood all too well. We all saw the abuse of free government assistance just by standing in line at the grocery store. There were plenty of opportunities to see people who didn't want to change or work for a better life. There were those who didn't want help but wanted a handout on the hard work of others. History seemed to repeat itself in families, as self-serving attitudes were passed down.

Many teachers were single parents. They knew well what it was like to provide for a family while meeting the demands of teaching. They, too, stayed up at night with sick babies, no one to help, and bills piling up. They were short on compassion, and rightfully so. Their success was dependent on students passing, but they had to show up and do the work to pass. Teen parents were notorious for poor attendance; some whined and expected a pass on assignments.

I quickly learned that not all students wanted help. They wanted a free ride.

## John and Mary

Mary was pregnant, not attending school; John was the boyfriend who asked if she could attend the weekly support group meeting. Mary was barely fifteen and by law should have been in school. John brought her to the support group meetings, and the students were supportive and encouraging.

The baby came in November. John was working and doing all

he could to provide, along with his single-parent mother. He was one of the most responsible young men I'd ever worked with. All the girls in the support group envied Mary for having someone like John.

Mary enrolled in school; the baby was placed in a very qualified daycare, but after a few days, Mary began missing school. It was the usual excuses: "I'm tired. I don't get any sleep. I didn't get my homework done." However, she took the baby to daycare while she went back home to sleep all day. The rule was: no school, no daycare.

There was a long waiting list for childcare assistance, and there was no tolerance for abuse of such a privilege or taxpayer funds. Mary continued to miss school, and John began to skip classes. The baby was in daycare each time. It finally became evident: Mary didn't want help; she wanted a handout.

Mary and John were both smart and capable. They came from single-parent homes, but so did a host of the other students who were thriving. John's mother was supportive; I wasn't sure about Mary's mother. As was customary by law, after so many unexcused absences, Mary received notice to appear in court. When phone calls from attendance clerks didn't get a parent's attention, a trip before a judge and a hefty fine did.

One day, Mary's mother found out her daughter was losing daycare as well as going to court for failure to attend school; she came knocking on my door as well as the school principal's. I had no idea who she was. She demanded Mary's daycare funding be reinstated and the attendance record be changed. That was not going to happen.

I wish I could say this ended well, but it didn't.

The attendance laws couldn't touch Mary if she and John married, but both sets of parents had to sign consent. John's mother called, angry and frustrated. "John is determined to marry her," she said.

John was distant and angry when I tried to talk to him. Like his mother, he was frustrated. His grades were dropping, and he was scared he wouldn't graduate. He was tired, both physically and emotionally.

"I love my little boy," he sighed, "but the only way to solve any of this is to get married."

Getting married meant Mary could drop out of school. His logic was confusing, until a few weeks later, when rumors circulated Mary was pregnant again.

From what I heard through the student grapevine, they married. John got his GED and joined the military, and I never heard from them again. I pondered the situation for a while. Finally, I realized it never was what anyone else did or didn't do; it was what Mary didn't do. Mary didn't go to school or participate in her education; she didn't invest in her life or future. Even providing childcare, transportation, tutoring, and counseling couldn't erase what we call a victim mentality. I sadly learned the free hand of government programs will never change a person's perspective or heart.

Examples like John and Mary tend to be what society believes and some daytime talk shows parade to a viewing audience. Everyone doesn't want to change, but often, the most unlikely person will surprise everyone.

Sometimes, it begins with something as simple as asking the right question.

# CHAPTER 11

## A Simple Question

"If it doesn't make sense, question it."

That saying was going to teach me more than I could imagine as well as change the life of a young girl.

### Annette

Annette was a fourteen-year-old, sullen, and skeptical ninth grader with two children, and she didn't want any part of me. We were alone in an empty classroom, and we just sat staring. I stared at her. She stared at the floor. Whenever I'd venture a question, she'd either give single-syllable answers or else ignore me with a bored sigh.

Several teachers said she wouldn't make it. One teacher asked, "Why are you wasting so much time with that girl?" At the time, I didn't have an answer, but something drew me to this girl. The odds were against her: messy home life, a bad attitude, and not just one kid, but two: I had other students who were more than willing to accept my help, but that day, I kept sitting and staring. She crossed her arms and fixed her gaze permanently on the floor.

Just as I was almost ready to give up, I had another thought. With much care, and almost in a whisper, I finally asked, "How old were you the first time you were molested?"

Her eyes darted up, and her entire body tensed. My heart was racing. I carefully reached across the table and placed my hand over hers. I whispered the question again: "How old were you the first time you were molested?"

Teardrops began falling onto the table as her words cut through the silence: "No one's ever asked me that."

As Annette's story unfolded, I learned that throughout her young lifetime Annette's mother had brought different boyfriends into their single-parent home. Annette was molested at the age of five. From that time on, life changed for her.

Annette had many issues she couldn't change; through the choices of another, she had been robbed of her innocence. Her life had been hard, and no one even knew what inner battle she fought because of that horrendous abuse. As a child, she couldn't control what happened.

If it doesn't make sense, question it. Kids having sex doesn't make sense. That day, sitting across from a young girl who kept others at a distance through her tough demeanor, a simple question broke through the barrier.

Why did I ask her that question? To her, I was just a stranger, yet I handed her a cup of cold water; it was her truth locked away that set her free.

It would take years for her to change, but with time, love, counseling, and support, she did. It would take hours, weeks, months, and even years for her to learn to trust, but that day was the starting point.

No one could go back and right the wrong. She had to begin where she was. The one thing she controlled was choosing to stay in school. She saw the choices: drop out of school, become dependent on welfare, and live like the rest of her family. The other option was to stay in school, graduate, and explore all the possibilities that education provides.

She fought a hard, uphill battle. Our thinking doesn't miraculously change; old ways and habits that have ruled our lives have to be replaced with healthy choices. By the time Annette graduated, there was a third baby. When I heard she was pregnant again, I was disappointed and wanted to walk away. She was a senior and a leader in the support group meetings. I stood at a crossroads of decision: remove her from the group or allow her to stay.

Other teachers were now questioning the effectiveness of these group meetings. "Doesn't look like they are getting the message," one teacher quipped in the hallway.

I went home dejected and confused. I was so sure in what I believed. I was tough but fair with the students, and I believed, maybe to a fault, that they could change.

Recently, the students were stepping into a new arena in the fight against teenage pregnancy by taking their stories into the middle schools. Their message was plain and simple: becoming sexually active is life-changing. Their goal was to stop sexual activity, not encourage it. Annette had become such a vocal part of our traveling speaking group that her choice was now compromising as well as jeopardizing what we hoped to accomplish.

I talked to Phil. He shook his head. I withdrew to the porch swing, which was my usual place to be alone and think and pray. As I sat staring at the night sky, I kept thinking of that day in the homemaking room over three years ago. That was the day Annette began to find her way to a healthy life. She had come so far, but she had a long way to go. Her heart was damaged and was slowly healing. She was still operating in that old mind-set of looking for love in all the wrong places. I still believed in her. I knew it would be tough to keep her in the group, but I had to focus on the heart of this young girl. Her heart was good. The kids in the support group were watching me. So many of them believed adults saw them as throwaways who had no worth or value; they lived with battles and labels. How would I handle this without losing their trust?

I knew God had a plan for her life and was confident she would embrace that belief in time. Against all advice and criticism, I allowed her to remain in the group.

When we talked to middle school students, she was candid and powerful. However, when she softly closed with, "Don't do what I did and end up like me," I thought my heart would break.

Annette went on to graduate in the top 30 percent of her class. Several years passed without a word. One day, the phone rang, and it was her. "I have something to tell you," she began. "You know that hope you always talked about? Well, I found it; I asked Jesus into my heart."

She was laughing, and I was crying. We were both celebrating.

She and her three boys were living in a government apartment with no furniture, no groceries, and no money. "God will provide," she said. "I just wanted to tell you my good news." She hung up.

I called members of my church, and two days later, two pickup trucks along with several men and women arrived unannounced and transformed her empty apartment into a home. One lady in the group took Annette to the grocery store and told her to buy all the groceries she wanted. Before we left that night, we formed a circle around three fatherless boys and a young mother who finally found what she'd been looking for. The men prayed a blessing over them that would usher them into a life of hope and potential.

With the help of grants, Annette enrolled at a community college. With high grades and an associate degree, she continued to a four-year college, where she earned a degree in social work. She didn't stop. A year later, she walked across the stage at the University of Texas at Arlington holding a master's of social work diploma. She eventually got off welfare, became a social worker for a school district, and speaks to women's groups.

Annette, like Mary and John, represents the stereotype of teen parents. The difference between them was Annette participated in her life through hard work. Many believed in Mary, but she had to embrace and own their vision for herself. While it may seem that other people blessed Annette, the truth is that she blessed us.

It truly was a win-win.

# CHAPTER 12

## The Faces of Teenage Pregnancy

The stories are many; the faces cross all cultural and economic lines. They all share a life-changing experience, yet no two stories are alike.

### Sheila

Sheila was in the ninth grade when she became a mother and entered our support group. She had been tossed from one person to another during her childhood. She was African-American and light-skinned; one side of her family didn't want anything to do with her, after her parents were killed in a car accident. They resented the fact that she came from mixed cultures. Her grandmother threw her out on the streets when she was only eight, forcing her to live in empty buildings and eat out of trashcans. Someone turned her in, and foster care took over, sending her from one foster home to another. When she got pregnant at fourteen, her life became even more complicated. For a while, she lived with the fear that she and her baby were going to be separated.

Sheila only knew rejection from those who were supposed to love and protect her; therefore, she trusted no one. Like all of us, she wanted to love and be loved.

When she came into our group, she was one angry girl, but underneath all that anger were years of hurt and feelings of hopelessness. All she had known was failure; therefore, she believed *she* was a failure.

This was the era of state testing, and even if students had passing grades and all their credits in order, they had to pass a state test before they could graduate. Sheila was finally a senior; she had failed the test the previous year as a junior and once as a senior. It was May and the last time she could take it before graduation. She had gone to tutoring, and there was nothing left to do.

Then she quit. She just gave up and refused to try. She simply couldn't face another defeat.

Sheila had come so far. Through the safety of the support group, she found acceptance and her own voice of confidence. She was the leading speaker when we spoke at middle schools. She inspired anyone at any age. She had grown by conquering her fears and attempting things that challenged her to stretch beyond her comfort level. However, the challenge of this test seemed too overwhelming.

One of her teachers called me in a panic. "Sheila isn't going to take the test," she said.

Running through the cafeteria door, I spotted her at the end of the hallway. I began yelling for her to stop.

"It's no use," she yelled back, never even looking up as she continued walking. "You can't talk me out of this," she continued, waving a hand of dismissal. "I've had it; can't do this anymore."

Running faster, I caught up with her when she was halfway out the door.

I reached for her arm, all the while pleading, "Just talk to me. Please." Panic had me shaking as I breathlessly reasoned, "You can't quit. Not now. You've come too far." Leaning against the wall to catch my breath, I made one last plea: "Please hear me out."

With her body wedged in the door, half in and half out, she stopped. She never looked up but kept her head down. "I've taken it two times and didn't pass," she whispered, as if all the fight was finally gone. She looked defeated. She knew all about defeat and little about victory.

Years earlier, when I faced the GED and didn't think I could do it, one simple question kept surfacing: "What if you do pass?" Just like with Annette, the right question at the right time changed the course of history for both of us.

"What if you do pass?" I asked. "What then?"

She stood, contemplating the only possible answer. "I graduate," she reluctantly replied.

"Isn't that possibility worth one more try?" I shot back.

She took the test.

And she passed. The counselor gave me the privilege of telling her. Sheila graduated with her class.

What if you do pass? That was the question; she had to do her part. Armed with words of hope and a number 2 pencil, she went in and conquered it.

## Linda

Linda was a senior when I met her. She was beautiful; olive skin, dark hair, and dark eyes. It was not only her kind smile but her sad eyes that drew me. The baby was due soon, and because of her large size, she didn't plan to go through graduation ceremonies. She was embarrassed. We talked often. I met Bobby, the boy who wanted to marry her, and like Linda, he was a quality young person. They reminded me of Phil and myself at that age. Bobby was quiet; Linda was insecure. Guilt covered her like it once covered me.

Bobby approached the pastor of his church about marrying them. The pastor was hesitant and suggested it be a simple family ceremony. He conveyed the message, "I really don't believe a church wedding with a white dress is appropriate given the circumstances." Like another young couple years earlier, they were married under a veil of condemnation. History does repeat itself in the places we so hope it won't.

In time, I had the privilege of sharing God's love and the power of forgiveness with Linda. I also had the joy of seeing her graduate with honors from high school and eventually hearing her share her story and the power of forgiveness with an auditorium of young students. Linda and Bobby had family who loved, supported, and showed them unconditional love. That truly makes a difference.

Although I have too many stories to write within the pages of this book, it was the ones who chose adoption who taught me a dimension of courage and love that impacted me possibly the most.

# CHAPTER 13

## The Cost of Love

**Lucy**

Her name was Lucy.

She lived with her mother.

Lucy was a junior. She took accelerated courses, made all As, and was pregnant. If you saw her in the hallway, you probably wouldn't look twice. She wore glasses too big for her small face and plain clothing, trying to blend in unnoticed. The day was fast approaching that she would be noticed.

She quietly sat in my office. "I'm going to put the baby up for adoption," she stated, never making eye contact. "When I told the guy, he said it wasn't his; my mom can't handle any more, so this is best." Lucy carefully guarded her feelings.

She agreed to come to the teen parent support group meetings. There were two others in the group who were also going to place their babies for adoption. Although she was trying to keep this at arm's length, I knew the day would come when it would become close and personal.

The months passed. Lucy began to share her feelings more and was realizing how difficult this was going to be. But she had no clue what lay ahead. She had consistently referred to adoption as "the decision that was right" for her. She never allowed it to become personal. Although her body changed, and she carried a tiny person within her for nine months, she never called "it" a baby. I had never seen anyone so young maintain such control of her emotions.

On a windy day in November, it became personal.

As I gently pushed open the door to her hospital room, I could see Lucy sitting in a chair. She turned her head, and a smile broke across her face. "Hi," she said, as I crossed the room to give her a hug. "I've got pictures," she added, extending two photos.

I took them from her small hand. "She is precious," I said.

She smiled, nodding in agreement. "Yeah, I think so," she said, never taking her eyes off the tiny baby staring back from the photos.

The usual sparkle in her blue eyes was absent.

"I hope they let me take this donut cushion home. I didn't know my bottom could hurt so much." It was evident that childbirth was making this very real.

The door opened as her mom walked in. We had never met.

"Mom, this is my counselor, Mrs. Jimerson."

Mrs. Jones and I acknowledged each other. She looked tired. The baby was born on Friday; today was Monday. There was more than fatigue in her eyes. Lucy's mother looked wounded, as though life had dealt her a blow she couldn't quite handle. We sat quietly, with only the sound of the television breaking the awkward silence.

"I have to go to the bathroom." Lucy struggled to get out of the chair and waddled to the bathroom.

"I've seen the baby," Mrs. Jones whispered, staring out the window. "I took three rolls of film. I even made a note of all the features that are like her mom's." Her gaze never left the window.

She was silent for a few seconds.

"I went back this morning to take one last look, but they wouldn't let me see her." Her voice cracked. "I wish things were different; I wish there could have been another way. Lucy told me that most of the girls keep their babies."

Lucy had talked more openly the past few weeks, but she never let me know she was sad about giving her baby to another family. She had weighed the pros and cons and knew this was best for the baby. She never wavered.

Lucy made it slowly back to her chair as the door again opened. We all turned and looked as three women entered the room. Lucy's clear blue eyes became a cloudy haze; tears trickled down her cheeks.

"Hi, Lucy," one of the women said. "Are you ready?"

I was puzzled by the lady's chipper tone as well as her question. I wondered, how does one get ready?

Lucy nodded. "But I may cry," she whispered, and she cried. So did her mother; so did I.

The simple hospital room became a court of law, where history would be made as a tiny baby, unable to speak for herself, would have her future decided. The door, left ajar, allowed the hallway chatter to infiltrate the room. I quietly eased my way over and gently closed it. I stood listening to the woman in charge as she read each page of her document. Mrs. Jones sat, wiping her eyes with one hand, clutching Lucy's hand with the other.

As the woman read, my eyes began to wander, and I realized

the normal frills that usually accompany the birth of a new baby were absent from this room. There was no congratulatory feeling, no joy. I knew that somewhere, a couple was filled with anticipation, after possibly years of praying, hoping they would hold their child and they would become Mommy and Daddy. Days ago, those words were still a thought. Not today. Today, they were parents. The nursery was all ready; actually, it had been ready for months, maybe years. They knew this day would come, but they didn't know what it cost. Neither did I. Not until today.

The eyes of my heart were opening to the other side, the one I was observing. A large brown bear sat alone in the unmade bed; a single red rose lay on the pillow. There was a heaviness in this room as the reality that a girl became a mother too young hung in the air.

Lucy sat silently. Any minute now, she would sign her name to a legal document. She'd been writing that name many times over the years, but that day was different. The course of many lives would be shaped by that simple signature.

The pen rested beside the paper. Lucy leaned back on the pillow.

The woman quickly gathered her papers and slid them into her folder, and then with an added gesture, she stooped to speak directly to Lucy.

"If I can help you, please call me." She extended a tender pat, and the door closed behind her. Her voice was sincere; her mission wasn't yet complete.

"Wait," Mrs. Jones called out. "There's a pink bear in the nursery. Please make sure she knows her mother made this for her." Mrs. Jones placed a picture of Lucy along with an envelope into the woman's waiting hands.

"This letter, well, someday read it to her. We want her to

know …" Her voice broke, and she no longer fought the tears. "… we love her."

The lady smiled and gently touched Mrs. Jones. "She'll know you love her," she promised. "I have to go; they are waiting." The door closed.

Adoption was no longer just a choice. That November day, the veil of reality was pulled back, and I had a glimpse into that world.

I walked to the car in a fog of emotions.

I never doubted this baby would be placed into a loving family. What I didn't understand was the price of love Lucy paid. I knew she would be changed forever. Anyone who experiences pregnancy is changed by that incredible miracle of producing life. Young or old, planned or unplanned, pregnancy is life-changing. But Lucy was giving life to another family. She was their answer to prayer; she did for them what they couldn't do for themselves. And she taught anyone who was paying attention the gift of giving sacrificially.

My eyes trailed back to the building only a few feet away, remembering the two remaining people, now all alone in an empty room.

I looked at my watch. I knew Lucy was watching the clock in her room. The new arrival should be meeting her new mom and dad within minutes. Within minutes, she would be placed into the arms of the ones she would come to call Mommy and Daddy. She gave her life; she gave her family. Though she didn't know Lucy, she would always remember her.

## Life Stops for No One

Lucy returned to the hustle and bustle of crowded hallways, exams, and term papers. One day, I rounded the corner to hear the words, "How could you give up your own kid? I could never do that."

Except for the tears, Lucy stood like a stone statue in front of her locker as three girls, upon seeing me, slammed their locker doors and scurried away. "They have all the answers, don't they?" I said while wrapping my arm around her as we strolled down the hall. "Let's go get lunch," I added, and we left campus, classes, and mean kids.

It's amazing what a quiet, out-of-the-way place with good food and good company can do. We didn't talk much; through the years, I was finally learning to just give them a safe, loving place to talk. This was Lucy's life; she had to learn to live it, and she was learning to take the high road. There are some things easily explained; this isn't one of them, especially to other kids who haven't had an adult experience.

From that day on, I frequented that high school campus often. I checked in on all my kids, but the ones who chose adoption needed to know someone was walking alongside them, both physically and emotionally. They had chosen a noble path, and I knew God would honor them. But for now, they needed me to be there.

## What I Learned

In spite of our age difference, Lucy and I shared a very life-changing experience. We had both been teen mothers, but our circumstances were drastically different. Therefore, the choices were equally different. God remains the same. He, too, paid a high price for each of us. We are loved, we each have a purpose to fulfill, and we can trust that life isn't over, nor do we have to go to Plan B. There is a promise that says, "All things work together for good." How that is going to look in Lucy's life, I'm not sure. But I know it will.

## Moving Forward

Lucy was a senior the following year. She did well in school, graduated with honors, and became an effective speaker for abstinence. "I want to make a difference for other kids," she said in one of the meetings. "No one should go through this." As before, she was matter-of-fact in her logic, yet it wasn't her logic that touched hearts. It was her story.

# CHAPTER 14

## Reaching Others

The auditorium was quiet; no one really knew what was happening. Over six hundred middle school students filled the seats, while a dozen or more teachers and administrators stood along the walls. Assemblies had become a thing of the past, as crowd control was becoming harder to maintain, so speakers weren't usually invited; until today. Students looked around, wondering why they were here. This had been kept under wraps. On our end, parents signed permission slips granting an okay for our teen parents to leave campus. Administrators signed off; all was a go.

A sense of curiosity filled the air. The stage was empty, except for twenty chairs and a microphone at each end. Teachers kept their eyes peeled to their charges, occasionally snapping fingers at one of their troublemakers, all the while whispering with fellow teachers. Like their students, they had been kept in the dark.

After what seemed like a lengthy wait and growing anticipation, the back double doors swung open, allowing light to funnel into the dimly lit auditorium. Twenty teenagers in single-file formation walked down the aisle and up the steps onto the stage, filling each one of the twenty chairs. The girls wore their best dresses; the guys were equally dressed in their finest. All but one looked like normal teenagers. They sat, poised in their seats, eyeing their audience; a gentle quiet penetrated the atmosphere. No giggles, no whispers, only a deep hush.

Sheila rose and took the microphone. "Hi. My name is Sheila. I'm seventeen, and I have a two-year-old son." She passed the microphone to Lucy, stepped back, and sat down.

"My name is Lucy; I'm seventeen, and," her voice broke with emotion, "I placed my baby for adoption." Adult faces softened; the young audience was riveted to their seats. The mic was passed to the final person. "Hi. My name is Joanna; I'm sixteen, and I'm eight months pregnant."

I had been the final person, the only adult, who walked down the aisle with my students that day. After they introduced themselves, I explained our purpose.

"Several months ago, during our support group, these young people had an idea. They wanted to tell other kids what no one ever told them. Many of them have younger brothers and sisters, about your age, and they wanted to share with you what their lives are like. If you think this is the life you want, that you get attention, or even that it's glamorous or fun, they want to tell you their stories. Today, you will hear the truth from those who know it best. This wasn't easy; I have known many of them for a few years; some are new, but once, they were just like you. They had hopes, had dreams, and were normal teenagers. That changed in many ways. Thank you for being respectful; what they are doing here today required lots of time, work, and courage."

That day was the beginning of opening a new level of understanding in teen pregnancy prevention. Administrators, when first approached with our idea, were very skeptical, as they should have been. Their job is to protect all students while in the learning environment and to scrutinize all material. But our timing was perfect; sex education was being pedaled by groups that made money off the taxpayers and influenced the hearts and minds of young kids. The battle was being fought politically across our nation. Teenage pregnancy was the number one cause for dropouts. And as a dropout with no high school diploma, these students were relying on welfare. Programs like mine had been birthed into Texas high schools because of those statistics. But more had to be done, and these were the very kids who knew it better than all of us.

## Common Sense

One day during the support group, someone made a comment that would expand their thinking into another realm: "I wish we could tell other kids the things no one ever told us."

"Why can't we?" I asked, and again all eyes turned my direction. When I asked the higher-ups for a support group, it was like I had finally lost my mind completely.

"A support group? For kids who are barely passing as it is? You want them to miss more class time?" Nothing seemed to work until one principal, out of the blue, said he was willing to try it. We met in the homemaking class conference room. Kids sat in chairs, on the floor, wherever they could cram in. We talked about everything from school, families, jobs, health care, love, and dreams, to life after high school. We had a safe place to grow.

Within a few months, several teachers relayed that attitudes and grades were improving in some of their students who came to the support group. As I was passing the principal in the hall one day, he said, "I'm hearing good things about your support group. Keep up the good work."

I wanted to do the happy dance but decided not to. I just grinned all the way home. This was a huge breakthrough.

"We need to tell other kids what no one ever told us." I chewed that around for days, weeks, thinking about what that would look like. We had a program in Texas that all the schools utilized. Prison inmates came to talk to middle school and high school kids about incarcerated life. It was very sobering and hopefully life-changing for kids already on the path of self-destruction.

As we hashed over the idea in the group, I began to write out the basic things they would tell kids. It made great sense; what my grandmother would have called "good ol' common horse sense." And "coming from the horse's mouth," wouldn't they believe it better than coming from some adult? I knew we had to get this together in the beginning. There could be no mess-ups. This would be a one-shot opportunity if it was going to be effective.

I took the new idea to the principal. By now, he wasn't surprised at anything I asked. He just sat back in his chair with his usual "Now you have three heads" look. I was told, "I'll get back to you." When he called me in, he had some questions: What middle school principal is willing to chance this? Are parents okay with this? What if something is said that some parents don't like?

I had thought through more than just that. I loved the fact that they wanted to do something proactive, especially since sex education was forcing its way into schools. My kids were real, sincere, and the best possible messengers. I loved the kids I worked with; their hearts were so fragile that I certainly didn't want to put them in harm's way. They were already labeled, the focus of rude comments, and left out of normal teen events. Group assemblies were becoming a thing of the past. Holding attention and having students remain respectful had become issues in schools throughout the nation. I understood the importance of protecting all kids, but my kids were my top priority.

I had done my homework. I learned years earlier that when you present someone with a problem, you need to have a solution. A middle school principal was on board; parent letters were written and had to be signed before students could attend. The rough draft was in my now-extended hand.

He just grinned. "Should have known you were a step ahead." With that, he gave his very guarded blessing.

We were given a time frame of forty-five minutes for the assembly; challenged to hold the attention of six hundred middle school kids and tell them the truth about an adult subject, without offending or embarrassing anyone. It took awhile for the list of top ten essentials to come together. They were all agreed on, just not in the same order of importance. Personal stories had to be carefully discreet and shortened in the telling. Students had to learn dress code and professional-type speaking skills. Commitments to show up and follow the rules were signed.

After months of preparation, the day came. Twenty kids loaded into a yellow school bus and headed across town.

Nothing was the same after that day. Truth does that. It changes what needs to be changed. When our time was up, the middle school kids rose to their feet and applauded. I suspect they were clapping for the courage and honesty of their older peers. We were all blown away. I don't know what I expected, but I'm not sure this was it. Students asked teachers if they could talk with the speakers. Out of that grew another part of our program; counselors were brought in to assist with the needs that had gone unmet for way too long. Truth was surfacing on many levels. The door was opening far wider than I could have imagined.

Word circulated throughout the school district, eventually leaving our small parameter. Calls from other districts came, asking us to speak to their students. Out of that need, a video was made, along with a guidebook that could go into classrooms across the nation. It was titled *Children No More*.

We had come a long way. In the beginning, it was all about them. Not anymore.

Through their experiences, they were helping others. They had long understood a fact that many adults had discarded: kids listen to other kids.

"I heard them speak," a teacher said in the hallway. "They're actually better than the inmates we had last month."

I was speechless.

As teen parents, they were finding their voice in an often-clueless arena. They will never know how many kids they saved from traveling the road they took. I know God will honor them for standing up for truth.

# CHAPTER 15

## When People Listened

It's called the Green Room, although it wasn't green. Movie personalities drinking coffee, eating doughnuts, looking and acting like ordinary people; for them, this was a typical day. I felt out of place. For me, this was anything but ordinary. I had been in New York one other time, but as a tourist. This time was different. This was *Good Morning America*.

Mentally retracing steps from the past months to today, it all began with one thought: *We want to tell them the things no one ever told us.* Within months, a small group of young people were propelled into the limelight of recognition and awards. Newspapers, radio, and the Texas State Legislature were just a few; television interviews, beginning with GMA and Oprah Winfrey leading the lineup. What had gained national attention was a video, *Children No More*. It was their stories, their truth, packaged to go where they physically couldn't. It had captured the attention of a sometimes uninformed society.

I seemed to be the only one watching the overhead monitor.

"Also in this half-hour," Charlie Gibson was saying, "the

subject will be teenage mothers. Some of them are so young themselves, and they are often bearing children out of ignorance and lack of economic opportunity. In Texas, there's a program that is doing something about teenage pregnancy, using a formula it calls the Three Rs: Restoring, Redirecting, and Rebuilding. In a few minutes, Denise Richardson will take you through a typical day of a teenage mother, and then we'll meet the founder of this program who herself was a teenage mother."

Charlie Gibson was talking about me. I knew family and friends were watching back home in Texas; I wondered what they were thinking when he told several million viewers that I was once a teenage mother. I knew what I was thinking. For me, secrets lost their power years ago, but in our generation, such things weren't talked about, so I knew this was uncomfortable for some. It wasn't that long ago that I lived in the delusion that some things were best kept secret. Even now, as I reflected back over the last few years, I clearly remember the day I found the courage to share my story. Time has not erased the faces of those young girls still etched in my mind or the day they changed my life. That was the day I found my voice.

As a young girl, I made a choice that rearranged my life as well as the lives of others. The day I began talking about that experience equally changed my life and the lives of others. That was the day I traded shame for amazing grace and freedom from secrets.

And it all started with one decision; to talk about it. Now everyone was talking.

Denise Richardson, *Good Morning America's* field correspondent, and producer Sondra Aiken had called me, asking, "How would you describe a typical day in the life of a teenage mother?"

We communicated by phone for days. "Will one of your students let us follow her around and see what her life is like?" Richardson asked. "We don't want just another story; we want to show real life. Will you help us do that?"

I was apprehensive. Richardson was persistent.

It was evident that most people simply didn't understand. Charlie Gibson had even said, "They are bearing children out of ignorance and lack of economic opportunity." Watching the overhead monitor, I wondered where these ideas came from. The experts all seemed to share his view. Earlier in the makeup room, I met the expert who, along with me, would share in the interview.

"I've been so excited to meet you, "she said, extending her hand. "You know, I live in the ivory tower, and I love a chance to pick the brain of those in the trenches." She had a doctorate degree, a professorship, and was writing a book about teenage pregnancy. I had lived it; the kids I worked with were living it.

Teenage pregnancy had become a hot topic. Politicians sounded concerned as they talked about it, welfare jobs expanded because of it, taxpayers complained about it, and safe sex peddlers were doing well. Everyone had an opinion or an agenda, but as of yet, they didn't have an understanding about the young people who were changed forever.

In some ways, I was no better. I once thought I had all the answers; I thought I knew what a typical day was like for a teenage mother. I knew what it was like for me at the age of sixteen. But the young people I worked with day in and day out educated me. Like them, I had known about rejection. But unlike many of them, I had not experienced it from the father of my baby. Nor had I ever signed away my rights as a mother. I didn't know what it was like to be a teenager living alone, raising a child. I didn't know what it was like to carry a baby for nine months, give birth, only to give it away. I didn't know what it was like to lose custody of a child because the boyfriend's family had the money to hire a lawyer. I didn't know about sharing a baby with the father's new girlfriend. I didn't know about the aftermath of abortion. These painful experiences were just the tiny tip of the iceberg.

Daily, the faces came and went. Some students were younger than others; some were more overwhelmed than others. Some held on; some quit. But all were in way over their heads, and they were all scared. The experts never talk about how they really got there in the first place, but the teens talked openly about it. They said yes to sex, and there was a lot more behind that yes than ignorance and lack of economic opportunity. "He said he loved me, Miss," was one answer. "I felt special, like I really mattered," was another. "For the first time I belonged, someone really liked me." They all found love and acceptance in the arms of another kid; I knew about that all too well. There was a lot more to teenage pregnancy than the experts seemed to grasp.

After long talks with both Denise Richardson and Sondra Aiken, I agreed to help.

For days, an ABC camera crew followed Kim, one of our youngest teen moms, wanting to see what a typical day for a teen parent was like. Unlike a normal teenager, her day began at five o'clock and ended around midnight. During the day at school, her childlike face and faded jeans helped her blend in with other teens. Many of the teachers didn't know she was a teen mom, since her baby was born before she ever came to high school. And like so many teen parents, she didn't openly talk about her other life away from school. But when the bell rang at the end of the day, she returned to her world, where normal no longer existed.

By the third day, the *Good Morning America* group had

sampled life in the world of teen parents. When I arrived to pick Richardson up at the hotel, she came walking out with a stuffed bear in her arms. "I just had to take something to Kim, but this is probably to make me feel better," she half-laughed as we headed toward the other side of town. "How do they do this?" she asked.

"Some don't," I replied.

The ABC people now knew what it looked like on camera to be a teen parent, although they had yet to discover what it felt like. While following Kim around, they witnessed her honesty and courage to persevere. They saw first-hand that not all teen parents are looking for pity or a free ride. Not all of them whine, complain, or become victims. But it was at one of the middle schools where they became even more enlightened. Such scenes as the openness of the kids in the speaking group, standing before both peers and adults, allowed them to see that teen parents could now take a message into places no one else could. For the first time, they saw the impact of kids listening to other kids.

When the *Good Morning America* team left Texas, they were better informed on a subject that most had known only through statistics and reports. They, however, encountered real lives and real faces. Through the lens of their camera, they would show the rest of the world another side to teenage parenting.

At this time in my life, some would say I was living a dream. Others would be embarrassed to have the world know I had once been a teen mother. Once, I would have been too. But the very teens I set out to help were the very ones who helped me overcome those feelings of embarrassment. Their courage to speak out gave me added courage to stand before my own peers.

Before I met these young teens, I thought life for me was hard. In many ways, it was. But I had also learned things can always be worse. However, we shared the common ground of a painful experience. As a teen mother, I learned life is drama played out in a very cold world. Some get lost in the drama. I found a way out.

Experience had taught me that no one needed an expert. It's just that some of us have had similar learning experiences. That gives us the raw material to help others: to listen, encourage, and hopefully give wisdom over opinions or advice.

"I'll believe for you until you can believe for yourself," was my standard commitment. I knew they could make it, and I knew my belief in them, and sometimes my hand up, was all some of them had.

That's why I was in the trenches and not the ivory tower.

# CHAPTER 16

## Faith on Trial

Ivory towers don't really exist but especially in the world these kids lived in. It would have been nice to find a common normal. Generally, the only common thread was being a teen parent. I wasn't always prepared for the trenches; every day, each situation seemed to bring something new to the experience.

I was there to help them stay in school and graduate. More often than not, I was learning as I went. Annette, Sheila, Linda, and Lucy were just the tip of the iceberg in educating me. I naively believed that with a hand up, teen parents would do their part. John and Mary taught me that wasn't necessarily true. So daily I waded into the deep end of some unfamiliar ditch. I wanted to believe sinking and giving up was not an option on my watch, but the challenges continually became harder. How could I convince them teen pregnancy didn't define who they were? They knew my story; they knew how strongly I embraced faith, and it was faith that taught me to rise above circumstances. More than ever, I realized without meaningful purpose they would eventually settle for a lesser life. We couldn't change the past, but the present could change their future.

Then there were days that took the life out of my fight and made me want to pull the blinds and retreat into a comfortable middle-class life, with no teen parents and no problems.

I discovered there were experiences that would rip the heart and soul of all of us.

———————

Barbara graduated the previous year. Up until then, she came to all the support group meetings; she never had a lot to say but seemed to thrive, and her smile was kind, caring, and an asset that encouraged others. Barbara was always the same: good attendance, good grades, and had her life in order. The students always had pictures, and Barbara's little girl was beyond captivating: brown hair, clear green eyes, and a bundle of cuteness. When she talked about her little girl, her eyes and face lit up. She was loved, and it showed. There was no dad in the picture, but Barbara loved her enough for both mom and dad. She made sure her needs were met, and she was truly first in her life and world.

It was a cold night. Barbara and she snuggled in a cozy blanket on the sofa, watching a movie; Barbara fell asleep. The next morning, Barbara work up to find her still wrapped in that warm blanket. During the night, she suffocated.

A cousin of Barbara's called, asking me to come quickly. When I arrived, Barbara was dazed; family surrounded her, but no one could ease her pain. I held her in my arms; I had no words.

The following days were a blur; it was a nice service filled with family and friends. People went through the motion of trying to say the right things; some said too much; some didn't know what to say. People ate food, drank coffee, and sat staring into space. One by one, they left; a room of empty chairs, dirty dishes, and stale food were the only remains. The room seemed as hollow and empty as we all felt.

I was standing to go when Barbara made her way to me. "Mrs. Jimerson," she whispered, "I want to come talk to the support group; may I?"

"We will talk later," I said, putting my arm around her.

She abruptly pulled back and said, "No, I have to tell them something. You know how you are always telling us we need to use baby beds? I want to tell them. They aren't listening to you; they will listen to me."

For years, I pleaded with students to use baby beds. I even began to ask teachers and others to donate baby beds. Phil and I would go pick them up; we kept them in our garage, and when a student had a need, we would deliver the bed and set it up. Many of the students lived in low-income housing located in the roughest parts of town; during the daytime, I never went without a school resource officer by my side. But often, the only time Phil could deliver the bed was at night. It was not rare for him to climb three flights of stairs carrying a baby bed.

Most of the apartments were beyond tiny; the living conditions were cramped to the point that sometimes a normal baby bed wouldn't fit anywhere. The students were sleeping with infants who became toddlers, and the children's safety was at risk. We pushed the issue in the parenting classes and discussed the importance in the support group meetings, yet many didn't listen.

Barbara understood. Even though her little girl was older and probably wouldn't have been in a baby bed, she saw life through a new lens. For the first time, she got it, but for her, there was no second chance. Out of her grief, she saw an urgent need.

A few weeks later, Barbara came to the support group. She told her story. I have no idea how many children she may have saved that day, but I know she was heard. Nothing speaks louder than a mother's pain. Her heart was filled with grief, yet she exposed her pain to allow truth to speak out.

———————————

When I was writing this book, I had no intention of writing Barbara's story, yet it continually edged into my thoughts. I didn't see the purpose. Many years later, I can't remember this without tears easing down my face.

I had carefully written each chapter; had a precious friend edit it, and made ready to have it published. I procrastinated; the work wasn't quite complete, and as hard as I tried to dismiss this recurring memory, I couldn't.

Why tell this story? My intent in writing was twofold: to dispel myths about teen parents by giving them a face and a voice. I wanted to remove the stigma so adults and society overall would stop writing them off as a problem and see them in God's perspective. My second goal was to renew hope, encourage education, and develop a work ethic that would motivate them to rise above their circumstances and choices. The bottom line: God has a purpose and plan for each one, but kids experiencing teen pregnancy need us to come alongside. They need us to believe for them until they can believe for themselves. Three older women came alongside me in the early part of my journey and taught me that.

Everything I did and believed for these young teens was founded on my own faith experience. I didn't preach faith, but I attempted to embody faith in my own life and journey. I fully believed good can come out of all experiences, until I couldn't make sense out of one precious little girl's death.

A new struggle began. Normal days were no longer normal. I went through the motions of normal: meetings with guidance counselors and pulling someone out of an emotional ditch while feeling like I was sleepwalking through each day. I felt numb. I tried to keep my emotions under a tight rein. I avoided my own inner struggle. How do you hold onto faith when you don't feel like faith is holding onto you? I had questions; students had questions; I struggled for answers.

One by one, students would appear at my door. They had fears. "If this can happen to Barbara, it can happen to me. She is a good person." So the question that continually rose was, why do bad things happen to good people?

Through the years, I have read many of the books on why bad things happen to good people. The answer always came back to faith, trust, and eventually accepting.

There are some things we struggle to resolve; we are asked to accept and to trust. Does it make sense? Many times, not to us. That is the hard part. We want an answer we can hold onto that provides clarity.

Although faith and religion are to be separate from the public school arena, there are some conversations that shouldn't be swept under the rug. When I was asked openly in our safe place, the support group, where my faith was now, I had to answer, "My faith is what holds me, no matter what."

Years ago, I heard a story about a man who was distraught over losing his only child. He cried out to God in his grief and said, "Where were you when my only son died?" A gentle reply pierced the air: "The same place I was the day My Boy died: beside Him."

I believe God was beside Barbara's girl on the day she died, even though I will never understand; there are some things the human heart and mind cannot grasp. But this is also the crux of faith: to believe when everything inside screams, "I want answers!" It was at this crossroads where my faith stood up as I emotionally fell down. As an adult, I was honest and showed younger people no one had all the answers for what life hands us. But in all things, we choose the road we travel, and for me, I made the wise decision to choose faith.

Of all the experiences, and there were many more that space does not permit, this was by far the hardest. I haven't seen Barbara in quite a while. My desire is that her heart became strong again, and I pray that sweet smile returned. She will never be the same; that is a given. Losing a child in death has to be the ultimate pain. What Barbara did for others was priceless, and that is what I choose to remember as one of my precious memories.

# CHAPTER 17

## The Final Question

The month of May was finally here. I was perched on a desk in the center of the lecture room on the last day of school. Kids were talking among themselves as I scanned the many faces, remembering how far some of them had come. I wanted to believe that maybe I had a small part in helping them get to this day. It was a bittersweet day. Some of them had been in this group the past four years; they wouldn't be back in the fall. At one time, graduating seemed to be a distant light in the long, dark tunnel of their reality. Now it was real. Caps and gowns had been passed around; some squeezed the package tightly while others were ripping into theirs as fast as they could. Grins, laughter, and high fives filled the room. It was a day of celebrating what once seemed to be impossible.

This was a close-knit group of friends, a family of sorts. There were no labels, just real people who had found a safe place to heal hurts and renew dreams. It all seemed good, except for the fact not all the students made it. While the majority were seeing the possibilities of hope and a future, others caved along the way. I couldn't fault them; many didn't have a strong support system at home. I hoped they would return next year.

However, the graduation rate was higher among teen parents than in prior years, making the politicians who funded programs such as ours very pleased. Our kids had made a name for themselves in our community as well as throughout the state of Texas for courageously speaking truth to younger students. They were experiencing self-respect and enjoying feeling appreciated for helping others.

I was going to miss them; there would be others to take their place, but this had been such a monumental year for me as well as them. Sometimes, I didn't know who was the teacher and who was the student. Teachable moments happened for all of us. That is the nature of the world of teenage pregnancy; just when you think you've heard it all and seen it all, you discover you haven't. I did know there was one question left.

I had to set the stage; the question leading to the question: "Do any of you want your children to someday be sitting in a room like this telling his/her story as a teen parent?"

Talking ceased; shocked eyes stared. "What did you say?" a voice rang out above the shocked stares.

"Do you want your children to be in a room, much like this one, telling his/her story as a teen parent?"

"Mrs. J, you crazy? Are you on something?" Disbelief traveled from one face to the other. Bodies squirmed and heads turned to see if others were shocked, or if this was some kind of a smart aleck comment.

"You didn't answer the question," I shot back.

Riveting words in unison: "No way!" Their undivided attention filled the room.

"What will you do differently?"

An awkward silence hovered; they were speechless. That rarely happened.

I posed that question to myself years earlier, out of fear. But that one question caused me to look long and hard at the past, present, and future.

Being a teen parent is one of the most difficult challenges I ever experienced. I did not want that for our children. If that happened, I hoped we would face it with all the love, hope, and caring possible. But why meet challenges after the fact when there are things we can do on the front end to help our kids make wiser decisions?

"What will you do differently?" will involve different answers for everyone.

For Phil and myself, we wanted our children to know they were each special and loved unconditionally. My parents' generation saw that putting food on the table, keeping the lights on, and bringing home a paycheck was the best way to show that they loved their children. My emotional needs went unmet, causing me to establish wrong thinking about myself. When I was young and impressionable, I didn't understand. As I matured in wisdom and faith, I saw through a different set of lenses as to why my parents did the things they did, good and not so good. But we had the option to do things differently with our children.

There was no magic wand to miraculously wave. We prayed a lot. We learned to recalculate often, and I think we did a good job. Not perfect but good.

There is no way to perfect. Even with the best intentions, choices will be made, consequences will change plans, and second chances will be prayed for. But hurts, disappointments, and mistakes don't have to rob the hopes and dreams of anyone. That was my message to teen parents. It was equally for their children.

A new beginning could begin with them, but it first began with a simple question: what will you do differently?

That day, a new conversation began. It's one everyone should have. Whether you got life right in many ways, doing things in the right order, there will always be things that need to be put in or taken out of your life.

When I asked the question, "What will you do differently?" it challenged the students to evaluate ways to make things better for their children. If we don't ask ourselves the hard questions now, we will possibly face answering them in the future through lots of pain and "woulda, coulda, shoulda" thinking. "If only I had ..." doesn't cut it after the damage is done. We can all save ourselves lots of heartache and regret by facing truth today and making an investment to change what needs to change. I learned a long time ago: Time doesn't heal anything. I just carried my thinking from childhood with me; most of us do. Every negative experience along the way confirms our beliefs. Having a safe place, loving people, wisdom, and healthy affirmations in childhood can help avoid a lot of damage control later on.

We never know the question that will transform a person's life or change the way they think. The night I bowed my knees and asked Christ into my heart started with a question: "God, if you are real, will you show me?" The questions He led me to ask students through the years possibly changed the course of their lives. The day I walked into a principal's office and said, "Can we start a support group?" Out of that group came the question, "Can we tell other kids what no one ever told us?" Never underestimate the power of God in the form of a simple question.

When you ask the question, "What will I do differently?" you won't always get it right. However, that is a good starting place to do your part and let God do His part.

Then write your own story.

I did.

Thank you for allowing me to share my story and my journey with you.

Kathy Henigan Jimerson

# CLOSING THOUGHTS

"We want to tell people the things no one ever told us." Hopefully, we did. Through my story as well as stories of others, I hope you are encouraged to face your own challenges. Nothing is the end of the world, unless you decide it is.

"What will you do differently?" Begin your conversation.

Everyone deserves a chance to dream and believe there is a good plan for each life. Hopefully, you have insight you didn't have previously.

Teen parents may live behind a label, but they are kids who are trying to cope with one of the hardest experiences they will ever face. They are our brothers, sisters, sons, daughters, family, and friends. They need adults to come alongside them.

Two of the precious women who reached into my own hurt years ago are gone, but one is still alive. Because of their influence and unconditional love, acceptance, and guidance, we remained a family that withstood the tests of life.

I wrote my story as honestly as possible. I couldn't tell my story without sharing my faith because that yes forever changed my life and helped me find the real me. I hope when faith knocks on your door, you too will say yes.

Choose wisely. Give Him your hurt; He'll give you His hope.

CPSIA information can be obtained
at www.ICGtesting.com
Printed in the USA
BVHW081259110319
542310BV00009B/985/P

9 781973 653691